Eating Steve

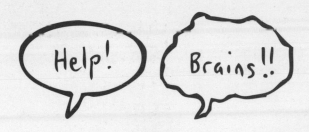

A Love Story
by J. Marc Schmidt

Published by SLG Publishing

President and Publisher
Dan Vado

Editor-in-Chief
Jennifer de Guzman

SLG Publishing
P.O. Box 26427
San Jose, CA 95159

www.slgcomic.com
www.jmarcschmidt.com

First Printing: October 2007
ISBN: 978-1-59362-097-4

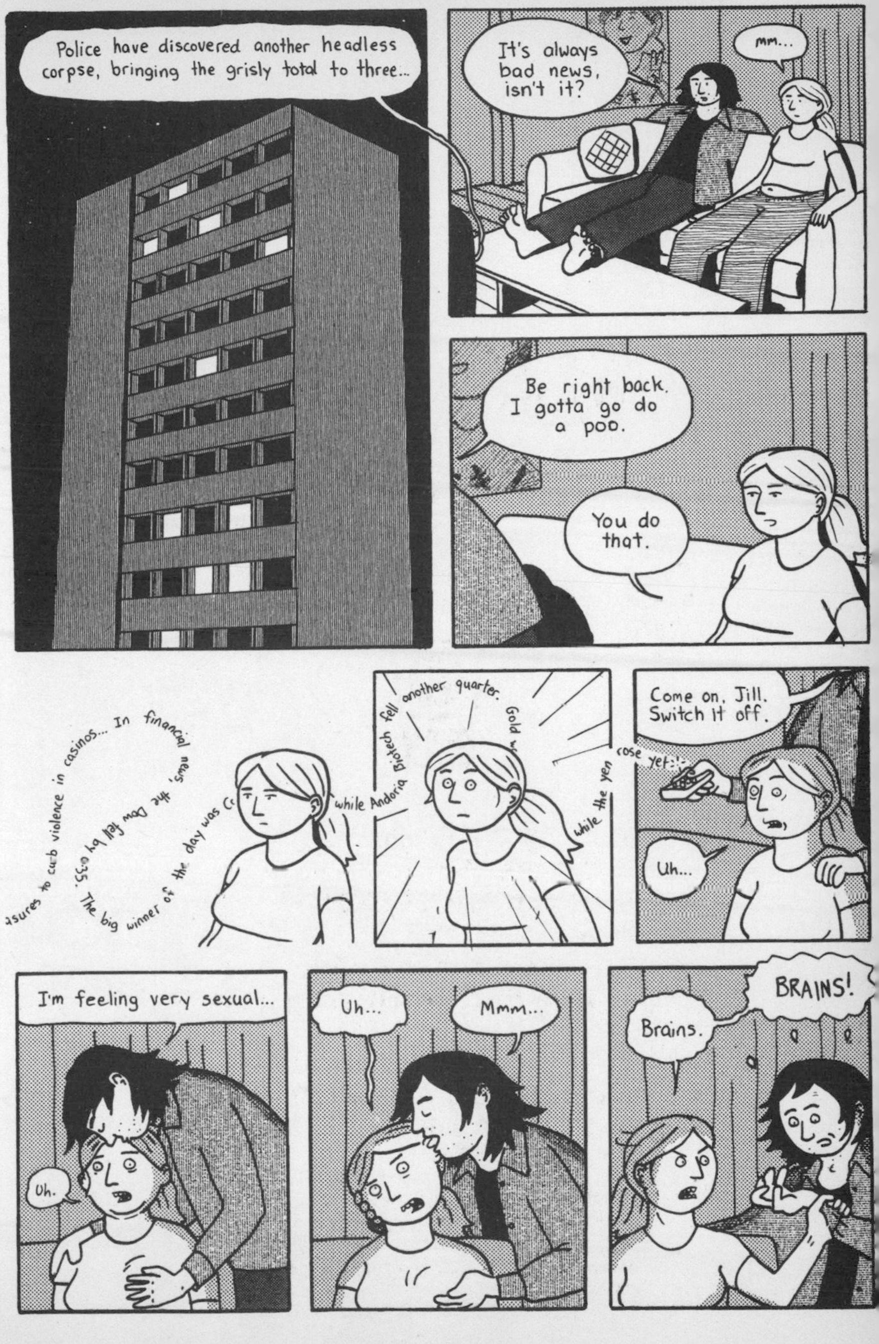
Police have discovered another headless corpse, bringing the grisly total to three...
It's always bad news, isn't it?
mm...
Be right back. I gotta go do a poo.
You do that.
asures to curb violence in casinos... In financial news, the Dow fell by 0.35. The big winner of the day was C
while Andoria Biotech fell another quarter.
Gold w
while the yen rose yet
Come on, Jill. Switch it off.
Uh...
I'm feeling very sexual...
Uh.
Uh...
Mmm...
Brains.
BRAINS!

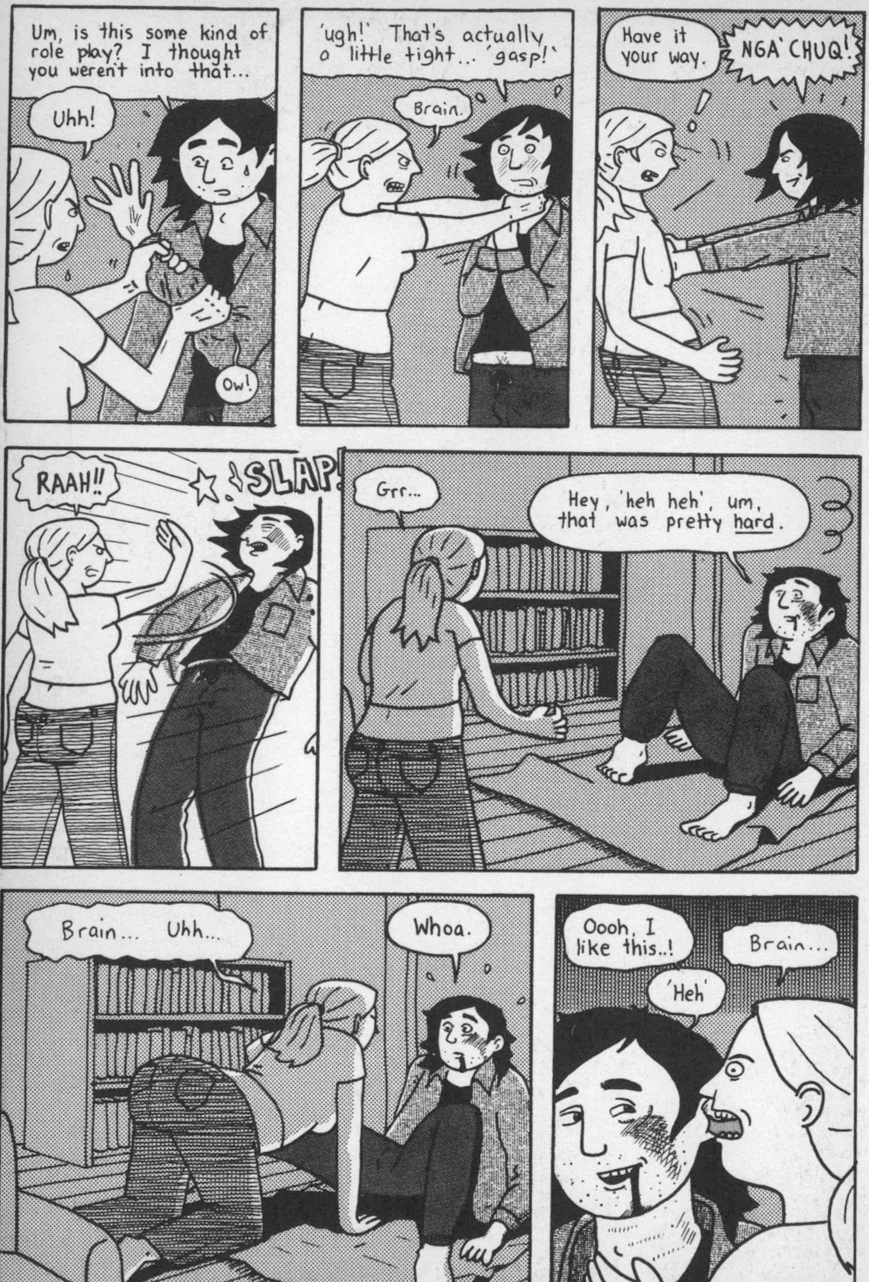
Um, is this some kind of role play? I thought you weren't into that...
Uhh!
Ow!
'ugh!' That's actually a little tight... 'gasp!'
Brain.
Have it your way.
NGA'CHUQ!
RAAH!!
SLAP!
Grr...
Hey, 'heh heh', um, that was pretty hard.
Brain... Uhh...
Whoa.
Oooh, I like this..!
'Heh'
Brain...

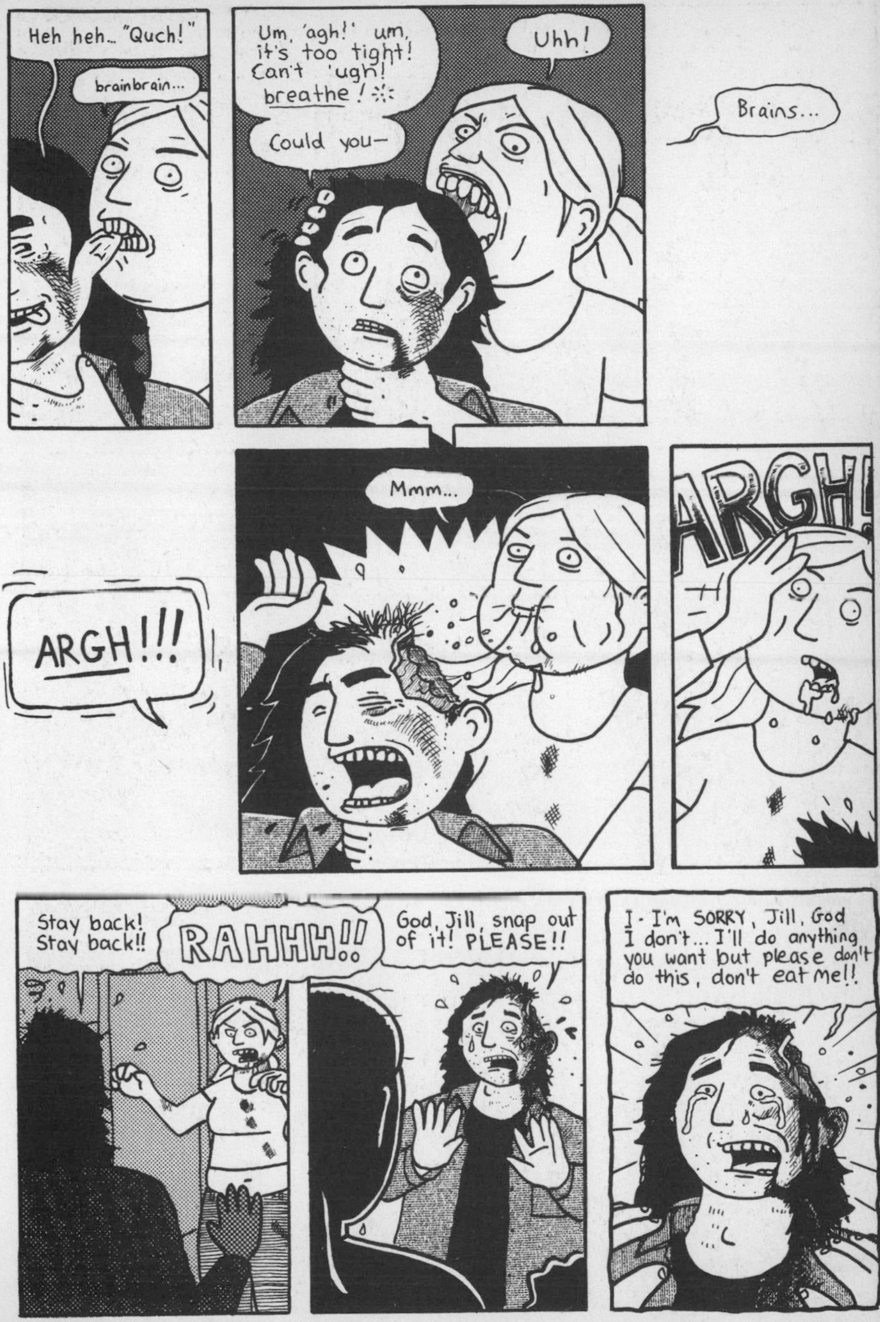
Heh heh... "Quch!"
brainbrain...
Um, 'agh!' um, it's too tight! Can't 'ugh! breathe!
Could you—
Uhh!
Brains...
Mmm...
ARGH!!!
ARGH!
Stay back! Stay back!!
RAHHH!!
God, Jill, snap out of it! PLEASE!!
I- I'm SORRY, Jill, God I don't... I'll do anything you want but please don't do this, don't eat me!!

Chapter 1

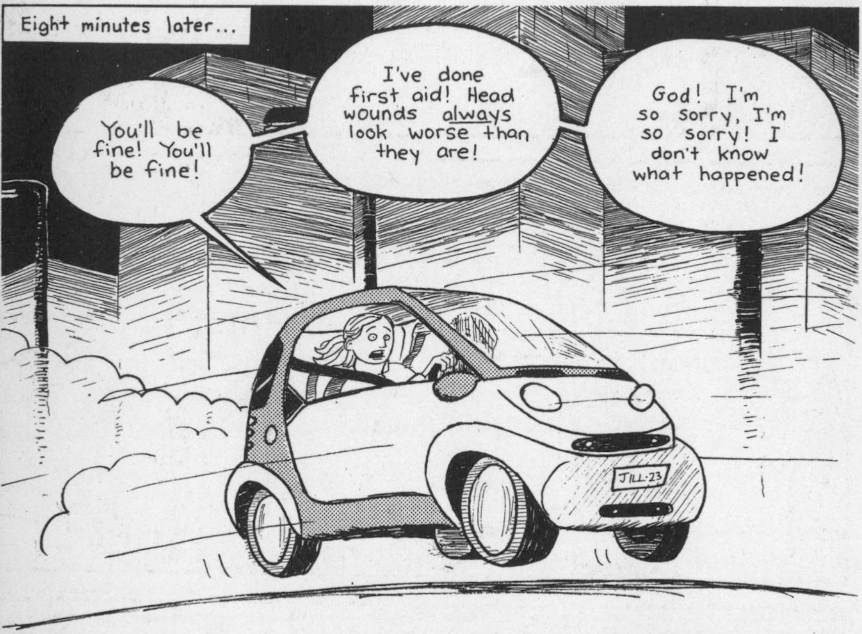
Eight minutes later...
You'll be fine! You'll be fine!
I've done first aid! Head wounds always look worse than they are!
God! I'm so sorry, I'm so sorry! I don't know what happened!
JILL-23

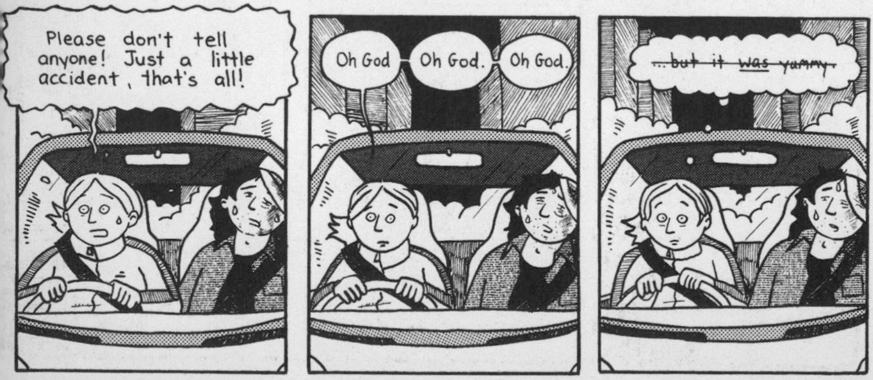
Please don't tell anyone! Just a little accident, that's all!
Oh God
Oh God.
Oh God.
~~...but it was yummy.~~

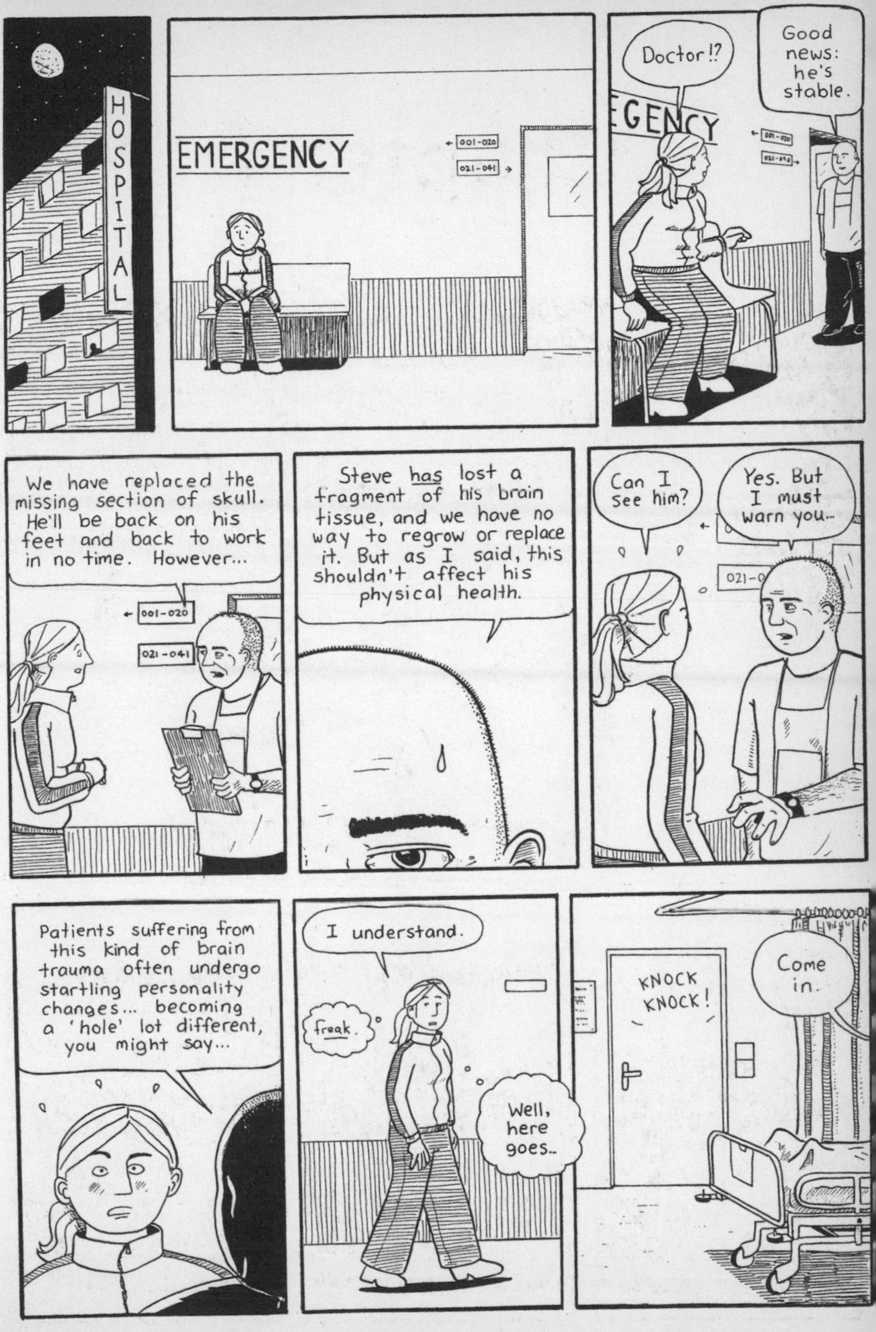
HOSPITAL
EMERGENCY
001-020
021-041
Doctor!?
Good news: he's stable.
We have replaced the missing section of skull. He'll be back on his feet and back to work in no time. However...
001-020
021-041
Steve has lost a fragment of his brain tissue, and we have no way to regrow or replace it. But as I said, this shouldn't affect his physical health.
Can I see him?
Yes. But I must warn you..
Patients suffering from this kind of brain trauma often undergo startling personality changes... becoming a 'hole' lot different, you might say...
I understand.
freak.
Well, here goes..
KNOCK KNOCK!
Come in.

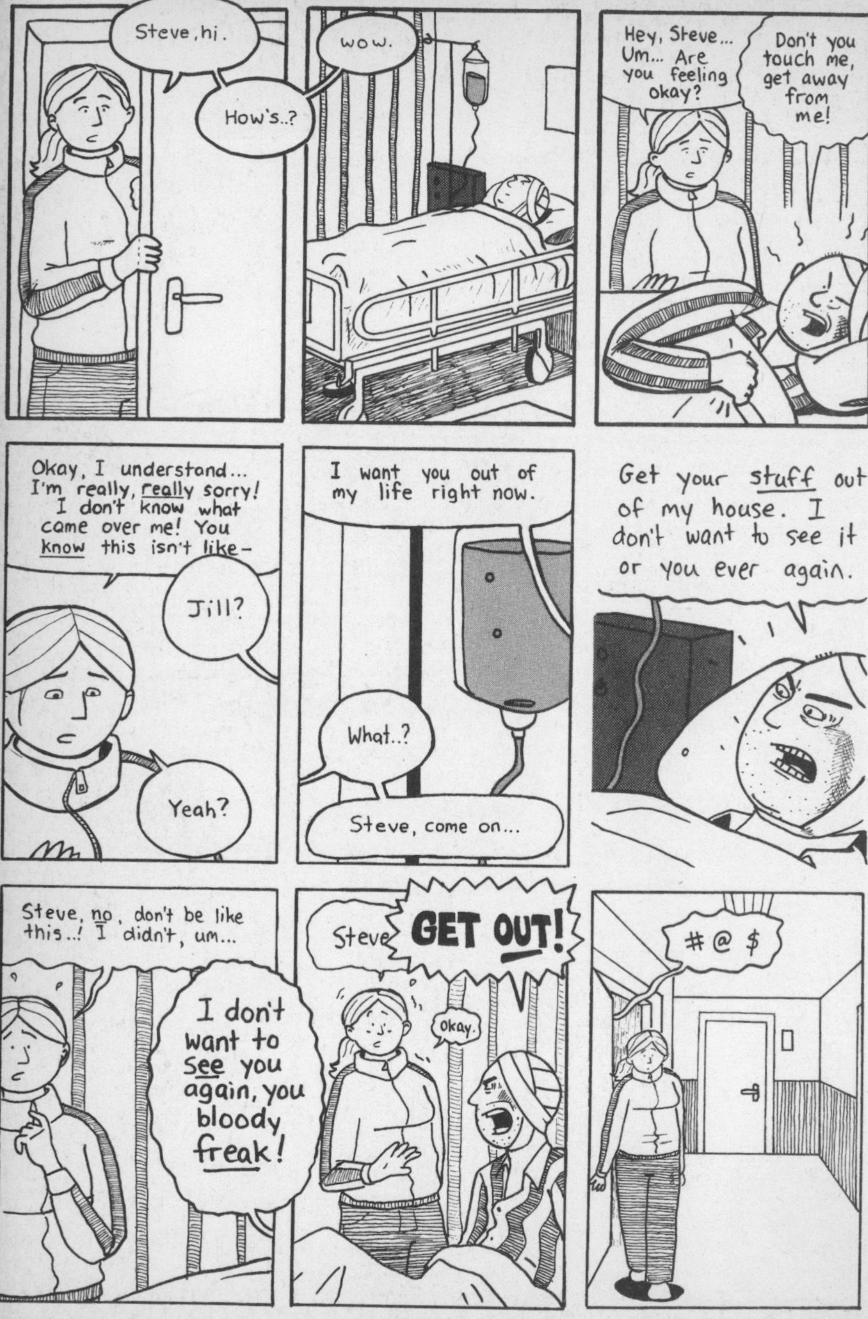
Steve, hi.
How's..?
wow.
Hey, Steve... Um... Are you feeling okay?
Don't you touch me, get away from me!
Okay, I understand... I'm really, really sorry! I don't know what came over me! You know this isn't like-
Jill?
Yeah?
I want you out of my life right now.
What..?
Steve, come on...
Get your stuff out of my house. I don't want to see it or you ever again.
Steve, no, don't be like this..! I didn't, um...
I don't want to see you again, you bloody freak!
Steve
GET OUT!
Okay.
#@$

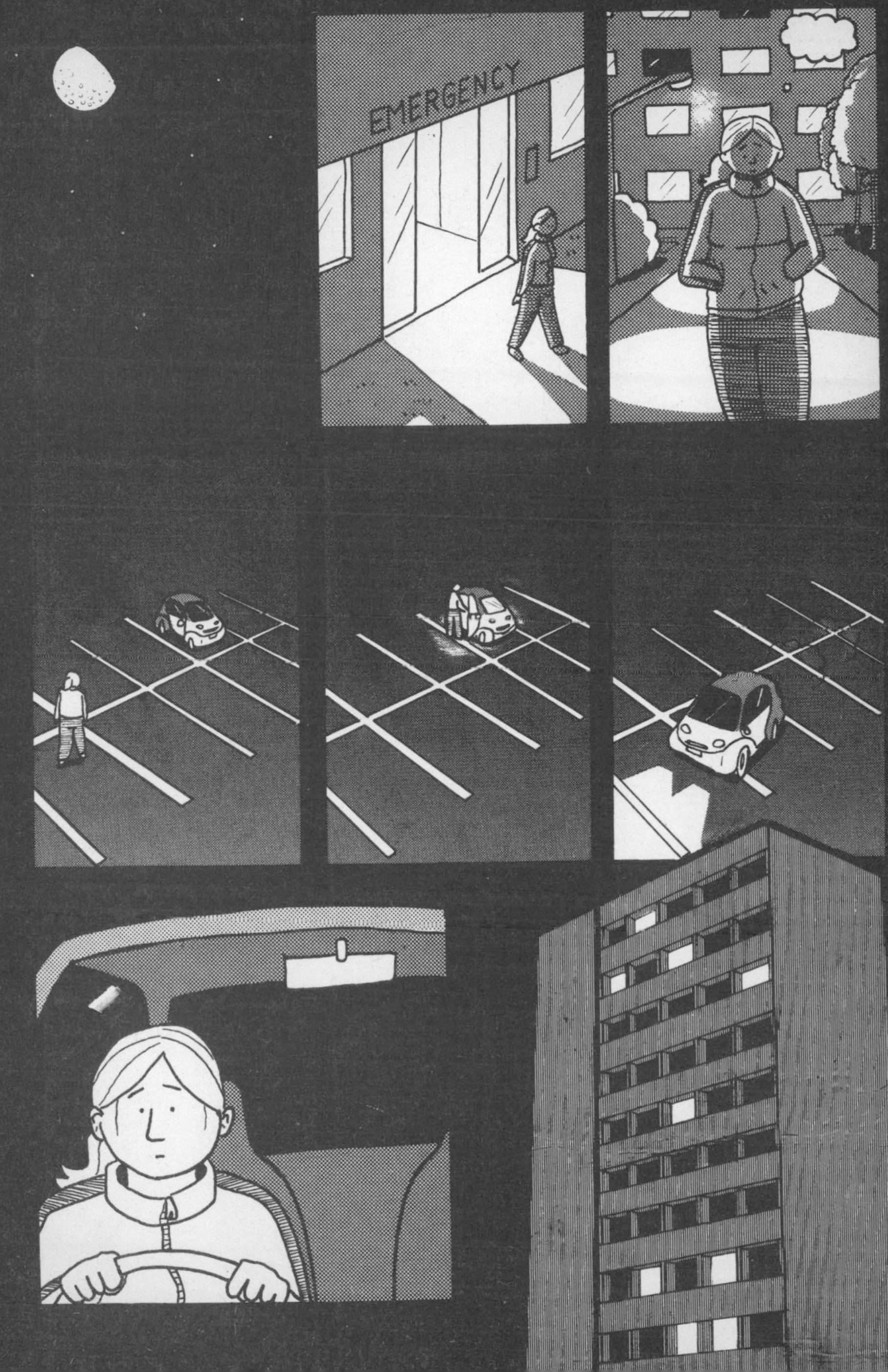
EMERGENCY

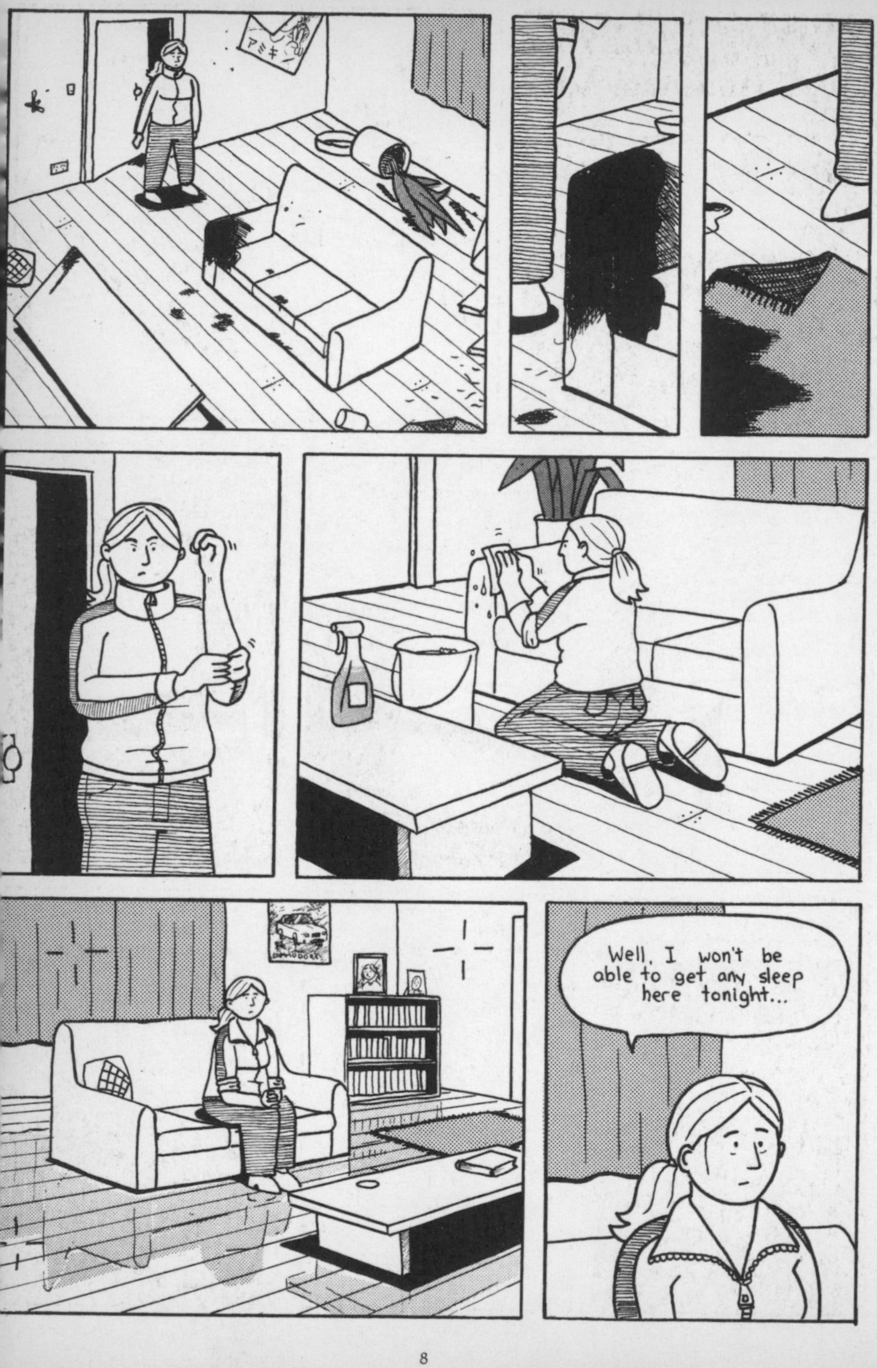
アミキン
Well, I won't be able to get any sleep here tonight...

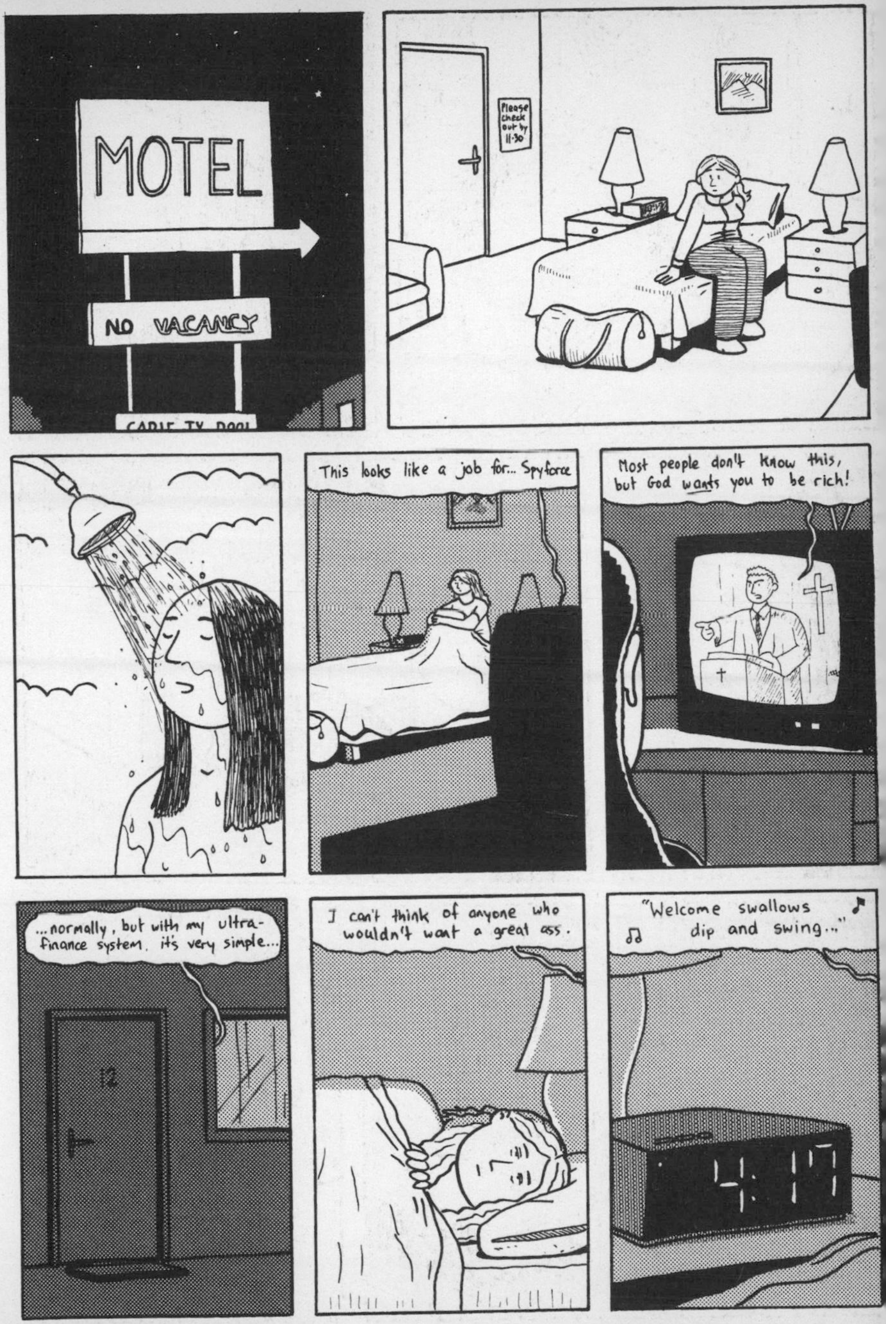
MOTEL
NO VACANCY
Please check out by 11:30
This looks like a job for... Spyforce
Most people don't know this, but God wants you to be rich!
...normally, but with my ultra-finance system, it's very simple...
12
I can't think of anyone who wouldn't want a great ass.
"Welcome swallows dip and swing..."
4:17

Jigglypuff: I choose you!
brr-brr...
Hi, this is Jill Fox... Yeah, I'm feeling really ill right now, so I'm going to take the day off... Great, thankyou... Yeah, I should be in tomorrow... Bye.
bip bip bip bip ...
brr-brr... 'CLICK!' Hi, this is Steve. I'm unavailable right now, but please leave a message, and
I'll get back to you as soon as possible.
BEEP
...
'sob'

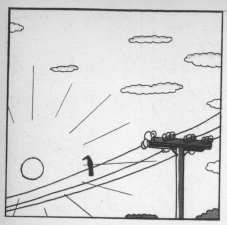

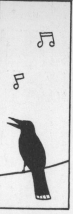

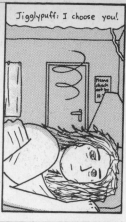

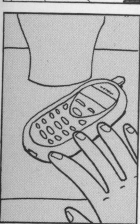

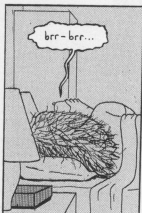

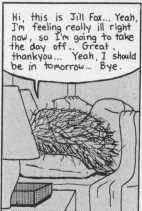

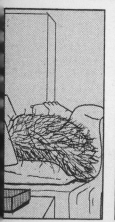

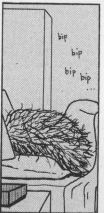

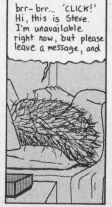

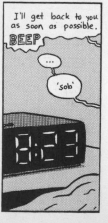

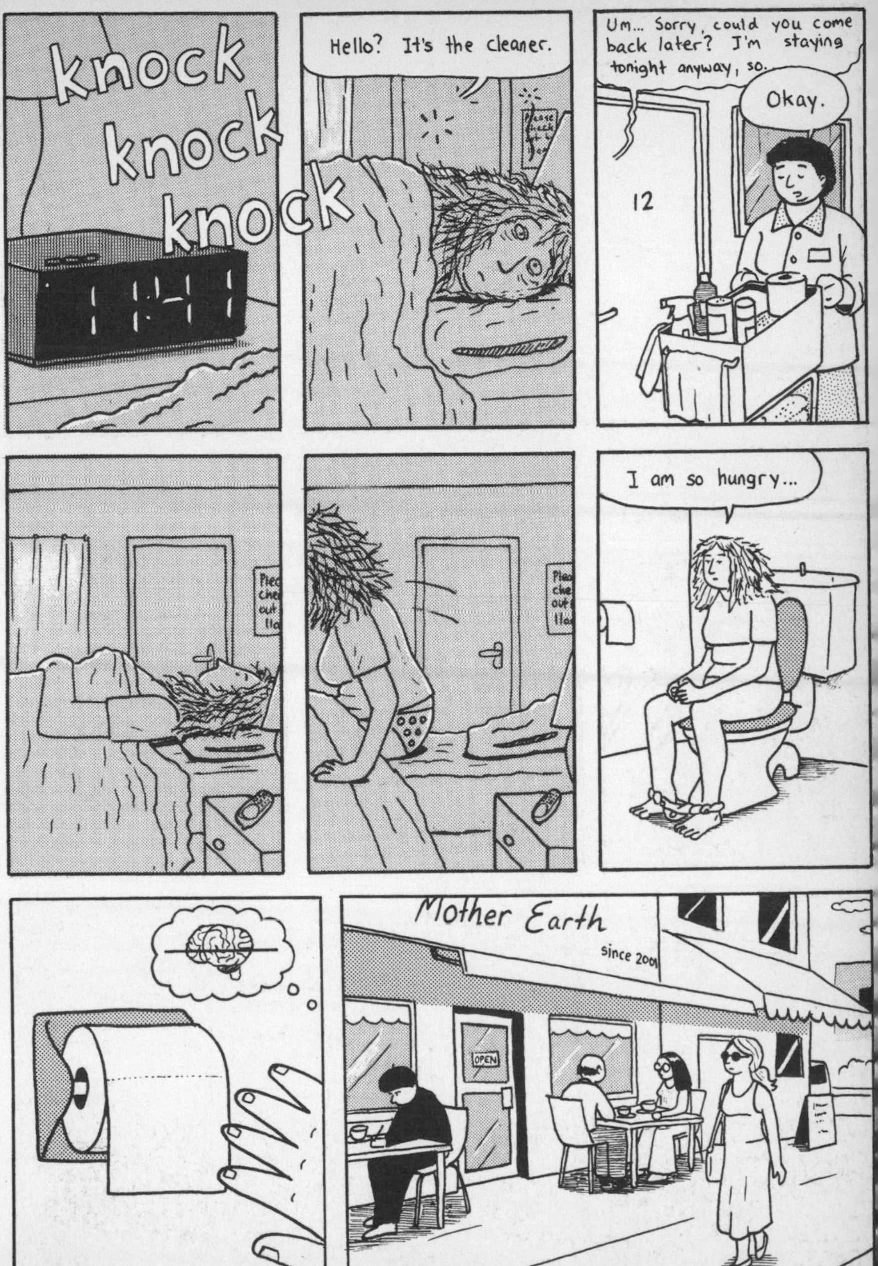
knock
knock
knock
Hello? It's the cleaner.
Um... Sorry, could you come back later? I'm staying tonight anyway, so...
Okay.
12
I am so hungry...
Mother Earth
since 200
OPEN

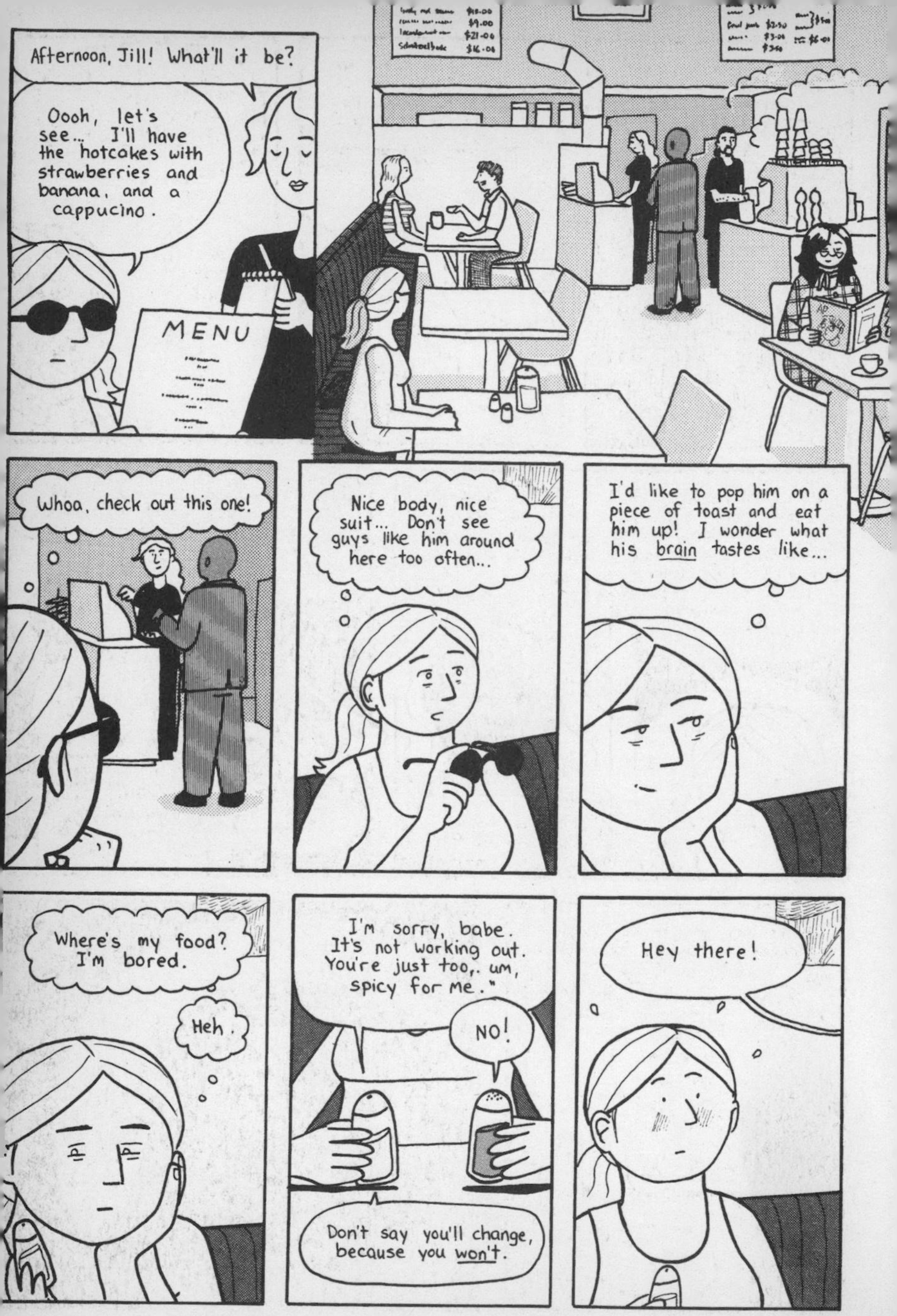
Afternoon, Jill! What'll it be?
Oooh, let's see... I'll have the hotcakes with strawberries and banana, and a cappucino.
MENU
Whoa, check out this one!
Nice body, nice suit... Don't see guys like him around here too often...
I'd like to pop him on a piece of toast and eat him up! I wonder what his brain tastes like...
Where's my food? I'm bored.
Heh.
I'm sorry, babe. It's not working out. You're just too,. um, spicy for me."
NO!
Don't say you'll change, because you won't.
Hey there!

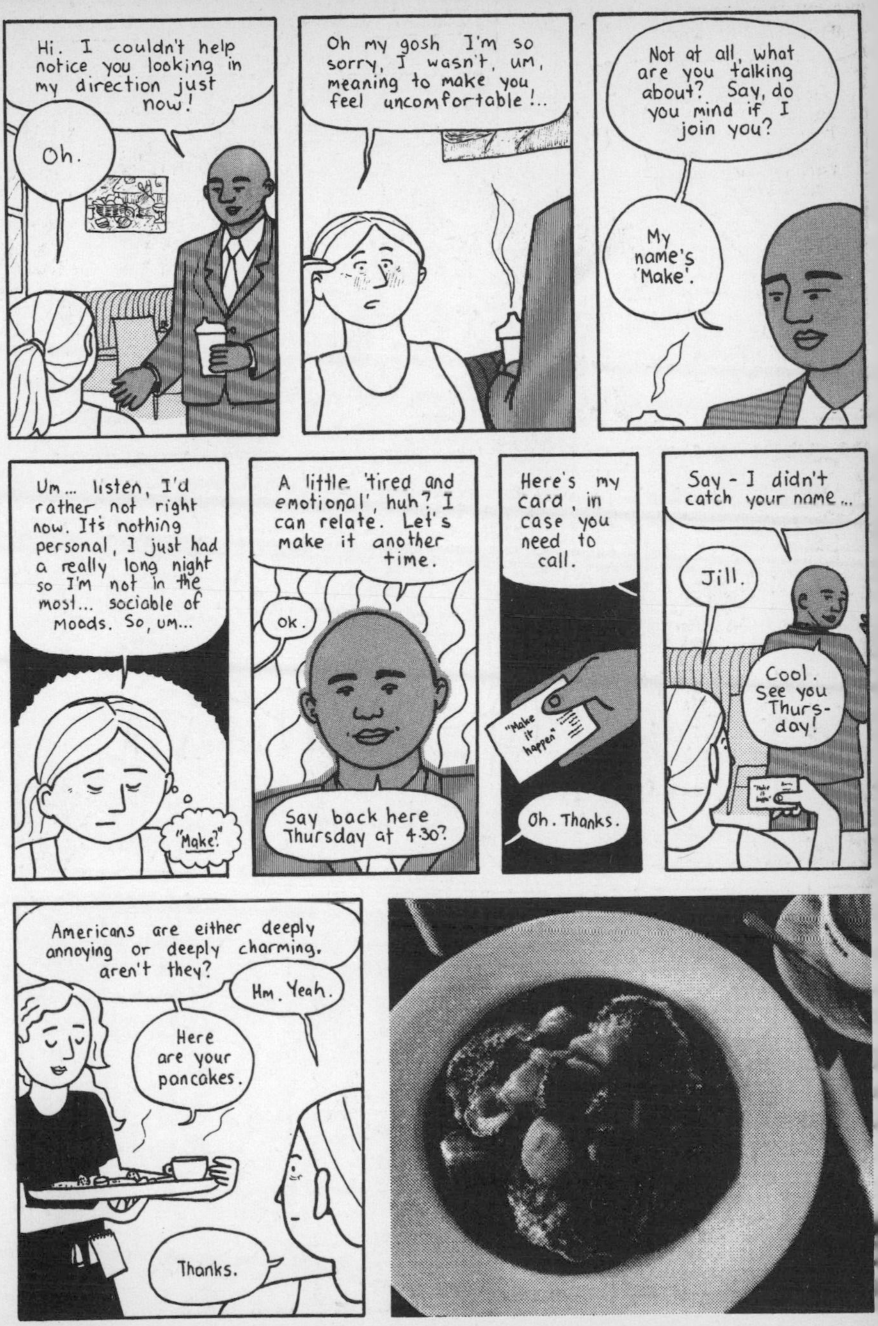

Hi. I couldn't help notice you looking in my direction just now!
Oh.
Oh my gosh I'm so sorry, I wasn't, um, meaning to make you feel uncomfortable!..
Not at all, what are you talking about? Say, do you mind if I join you?
My name's 'Make'.
Um... listen, I'd rather not right now. It's nothing personal, I just had a really long night so I'm not in the most... sociable of moods. So, um...
"Make?"
A little 'tired and emotional', huh? I can relate. Let's make it another time.
ok.
Say back here Thursday at 4:30?
Here's my card, in case you need to call.
"Make it happen"
Oh. Thanks.
Say - I didn't catch your name...
Jill.
Cool. See you Thursday!
Americans are either deeply annoying or deeply charming, aren't they?
Hm. Yeah.
Here are your pancakes.
Thanks.

Well guys, I finally did it...

I finally had the surgery to become a *centaur*.

MOTEL

And let me tell you — it's *great*!

The number one benefit is that I can *run* really fast. I can run away from *anybody* now, baby!

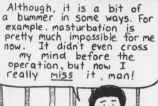

Plus, it's a talking point at parties, you know? It's wa

Hi, this is Steve. I'm unavailable right now, but please leave a message and I'll get—

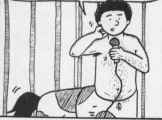

Although, it is a bit of a bummer in some ways. For example, masturbation is pretty much impossible for me now. It didn't even cross my mind before the operation, but now I really *miss* it, man!

And forget about meaningful employment! It's either pulling wagons or the *circus*.

I can't drive a *car*, either... Come to think about it, this kind of--

Hey! What the..!

When I get my hands on that genetic engineer...

It'd be funnier if it were a *real* centaur...

14

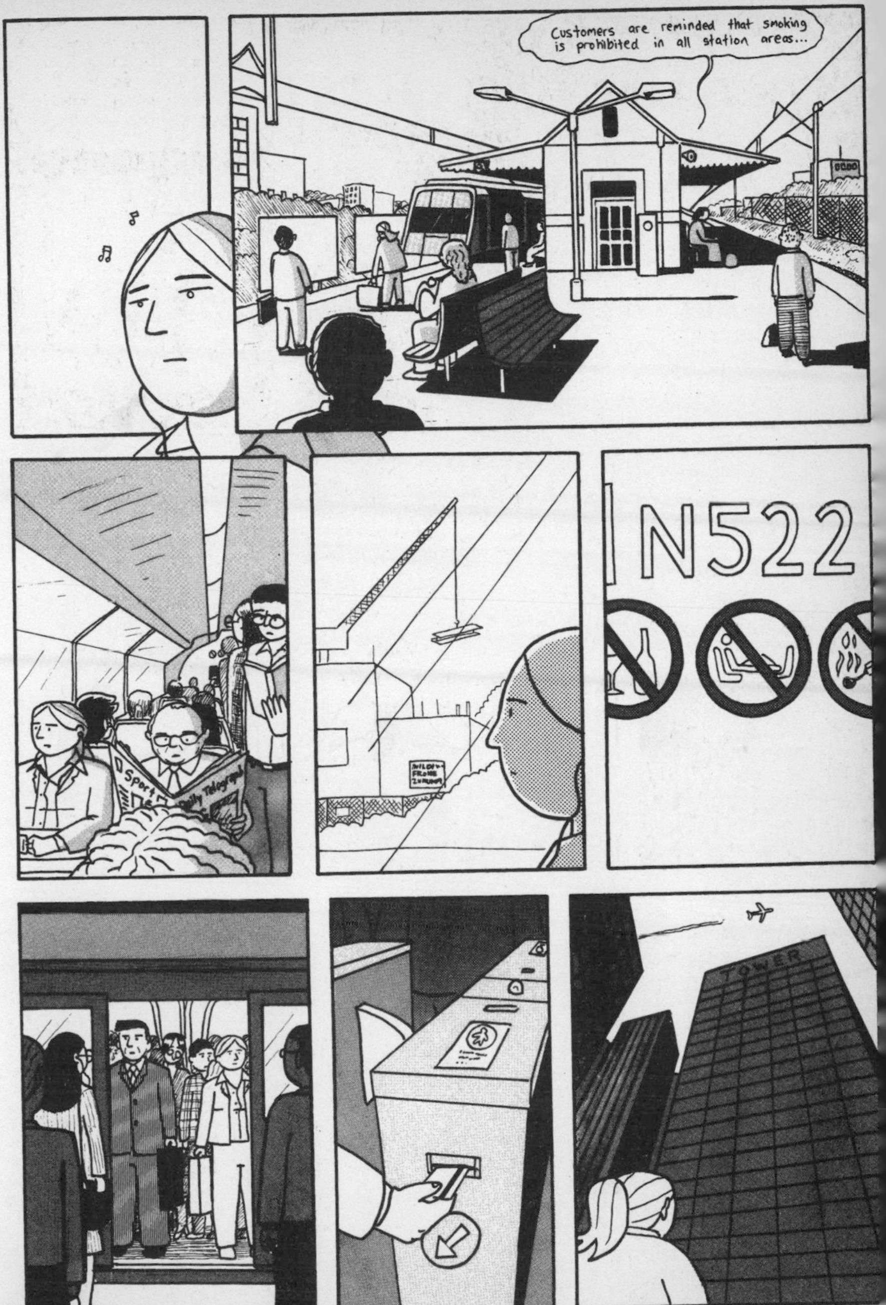

Customers are reminded that smoking is prohibited in all station areas...
Daily Telegraph
Sport
N522
TOWER

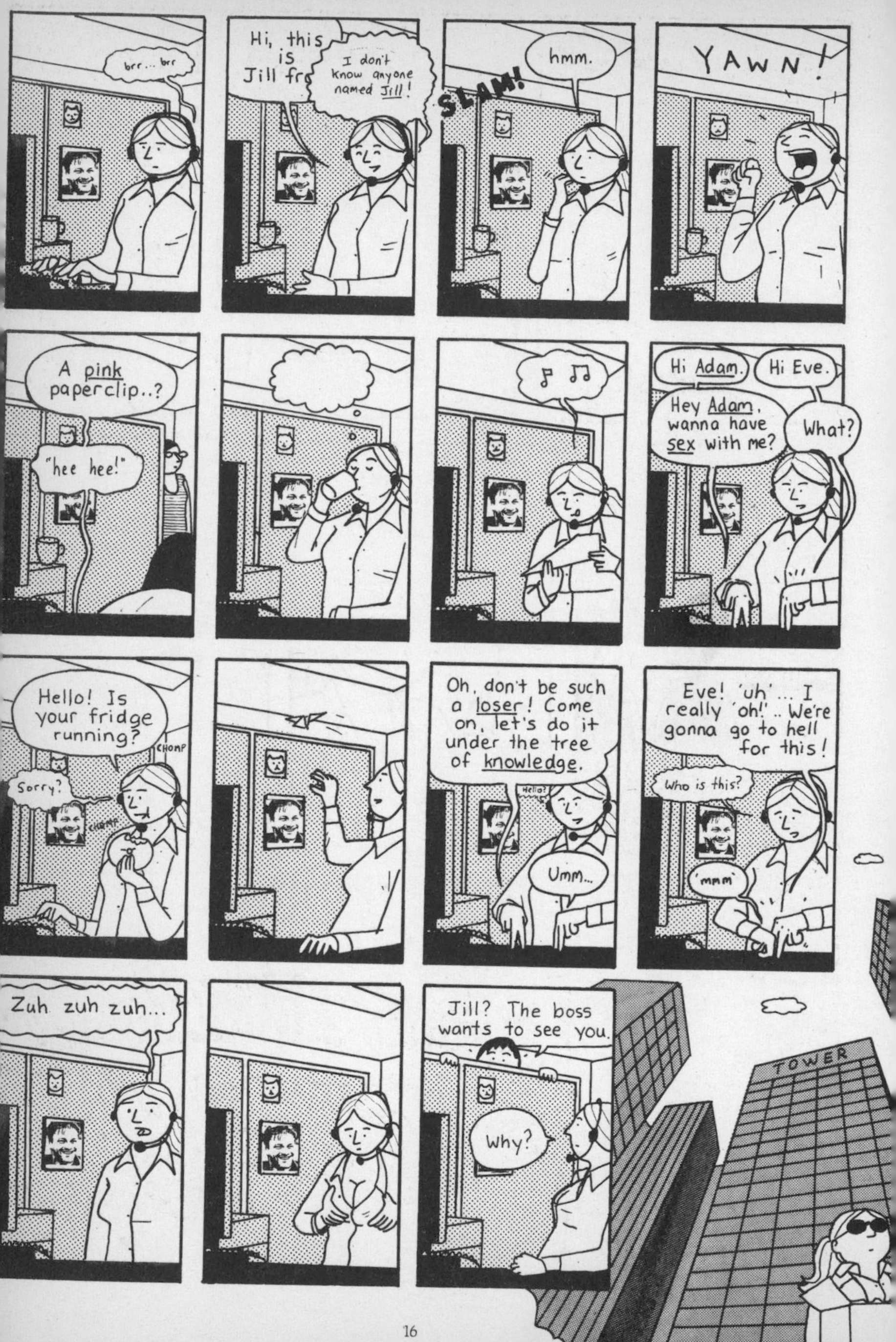
brr... brr
Hi, this is Jill fr
I don't know anyone named Jill!
SLAM!
hmm.
YAWN!
A pink paperclip..?
"hee hee!"
Hi Adam.
Hi Eve.
Hey Adam, wanna have sex with me?
What?
Hello! Is your fridge running?
CHOMP
Sorry?
CHOMP
Oh, don't be such a loser! Come on, let's do it under the tree of knowledge.
Hello?
Umm...
Eve! 'uh'... I really 'oh!'.. We're gonna go to hell for this!
Who is this?
'mmm'
Zuh zuh zuh...
Jill? The boss wants to see you.
Why?
TOWER

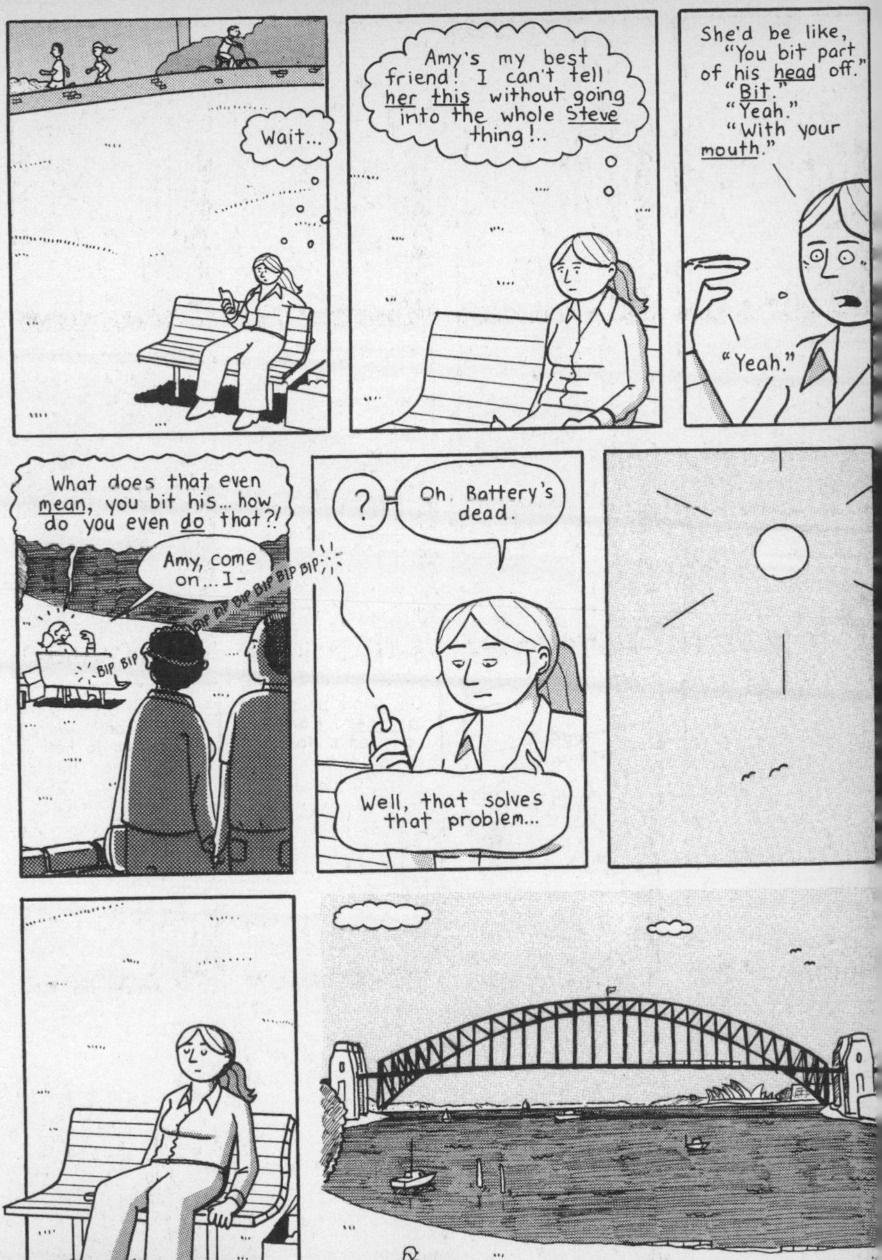
Wait...
Amy's my best friend! I can't tell her this without going into the whole Steve thing!..
She'd be like, "You bit part of his head off."
"Bit."
"Yeah."
"With your mouth."
"Yeah."
What does that even mean, you bit his... how do you even do that?!
Amy, come on... I-
BIP BIP BIP BIP BIP BIP
BIP BIP
?
Oh. Battery's dead.
Well, that solves that problem...

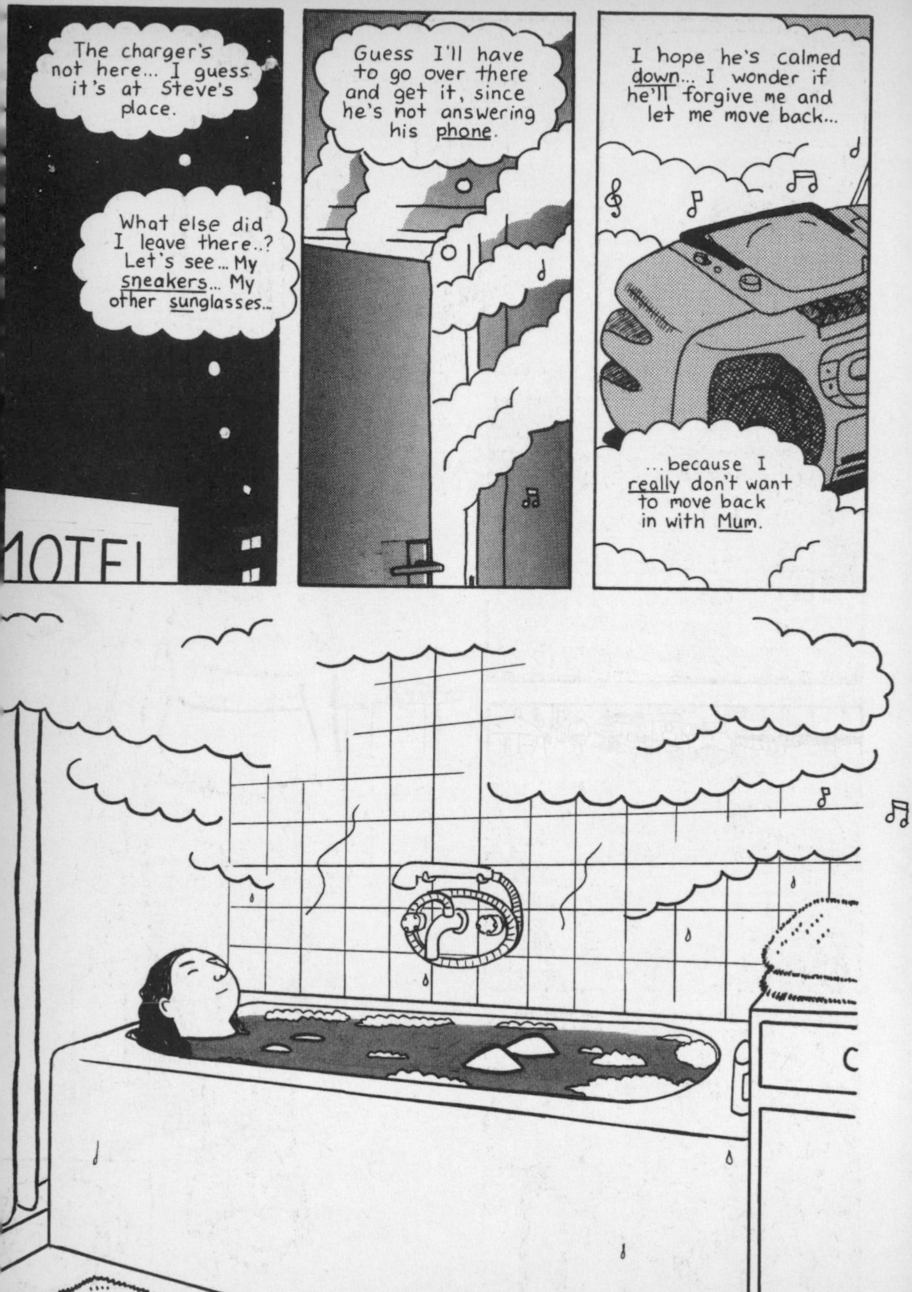
The charger's not here... I guess it's at Steve's place.
What else did I leave there..? Let's see... My sneakers... My other sunglasses...
MOTEL
Guess I'll have to go over there and get it, since he's not answering his phone.
I hope he's calmed down... I wonder if he'll forgive me and let me move back...
...because I really don't want to move back in with Mum.

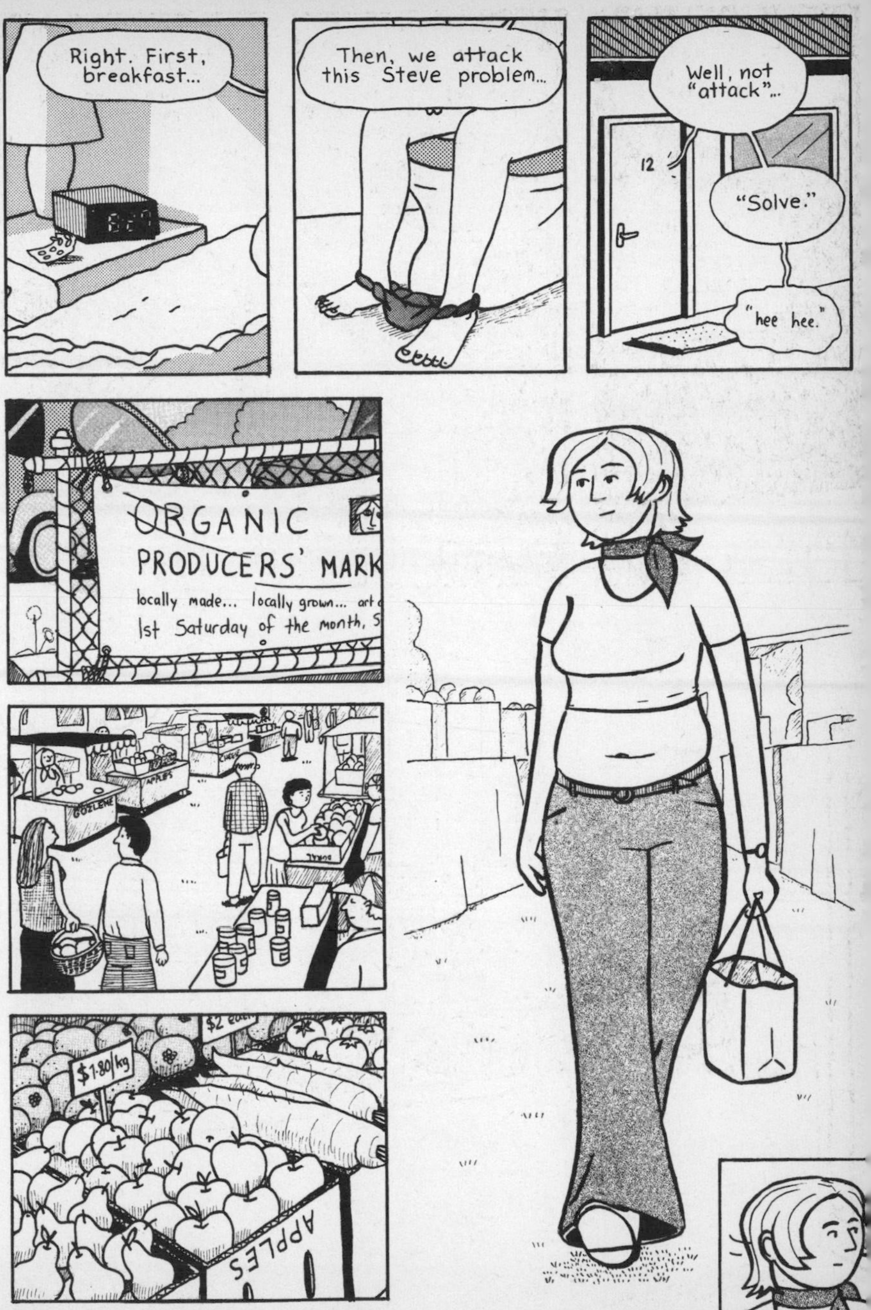
Right. First, breakfast...
Then, we attack this Steve problem...
Well, not "attack"...
"Solve."
"hee hee."
12
ORGANIC
PRODUCERS' MARK
locally made... locally grown... art
1st Saturday of the month,
GOZLEME
APPLES
CHEESE
$1.80/kg
$2 each
APPLES

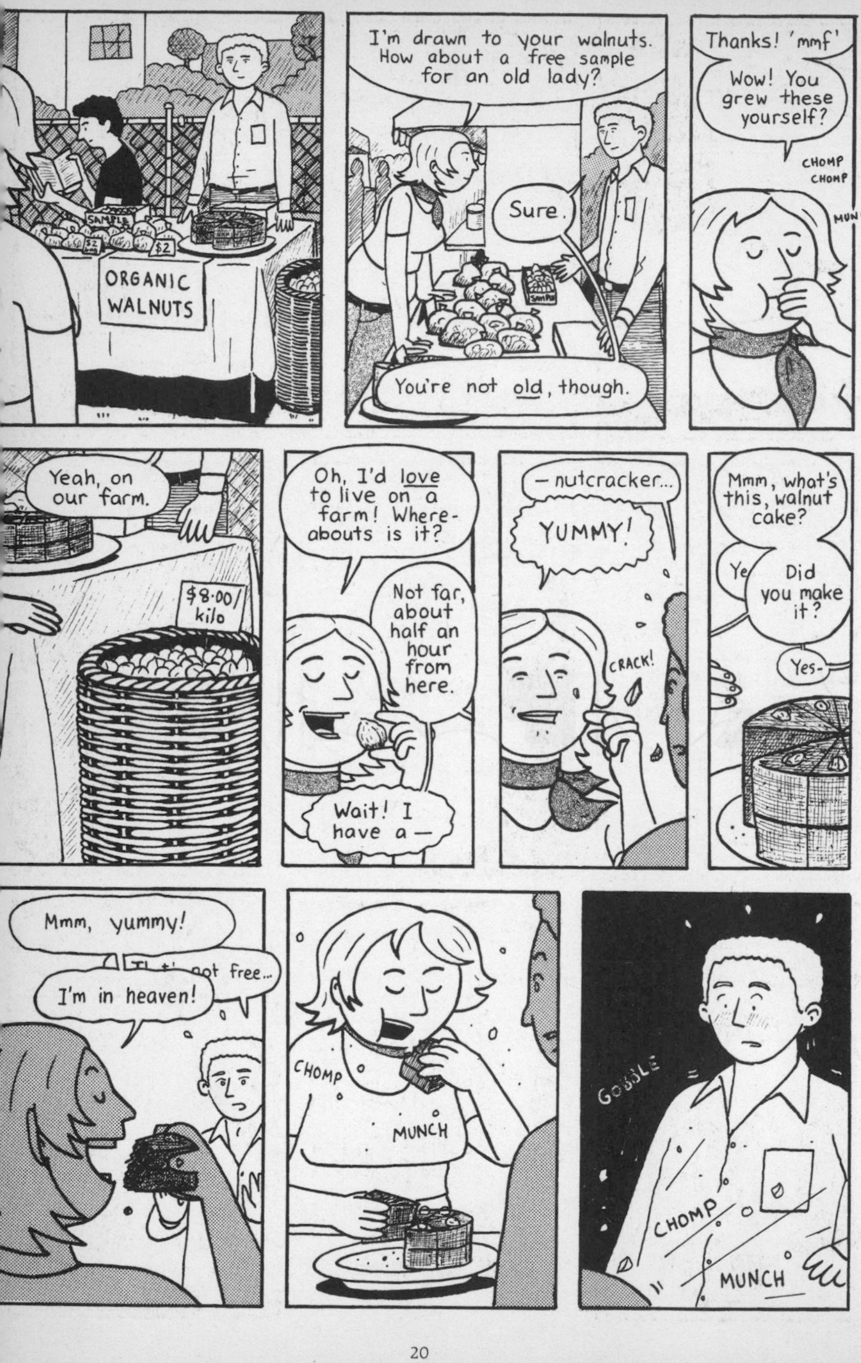
SAMPLE
$2
$2
ORGANIC WALNUTS
I'm drawn to your walnuts. How about a free sample for an old lady?
Sure.
You're not old, though.
Thanks! 'mmf'
Wow! You grew these yourself?
CHOMP
CHOMP
MUNCH
Yeah, on our farm.
$8.00/ kilo
Oh, I'd love to live on a farm! Whereabouts is it?
Not far, about half an hour from here.
Wait! I have a—
—nutcracker...
YUMMY!
CRACK!
Mmm, what's this, walnut cake?
Ye
Did you make it?
Yes-
Mmm, yummy!
not free...
I'm in heaven!
CHOMP
MUNCH
GOBBLE
CHOMP
MUNCH

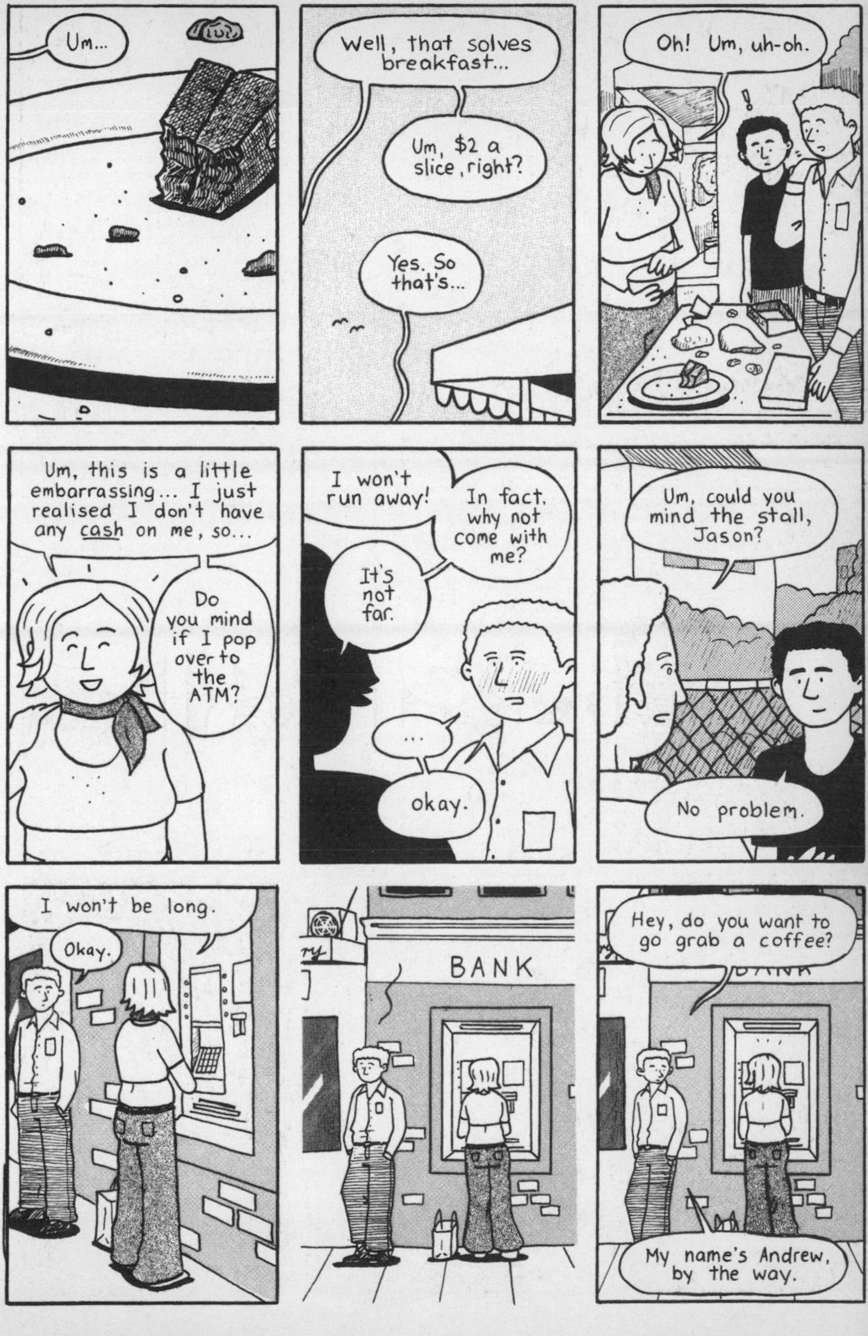
Um...
Well, that solves breakfast...
Um, $2 a slice, right?
Yes. So that's...
Oh! Um, uh-oh.
!
Um, this is a little embarrassing... I just realised I don't have any cash on me, so...
Do you mind if I pop over to the ATM?
I won't run away!
In fact, why not come with me?
It's not far.
...
okay.
Um, could you mind the stall, Jason?
No problem.
I won't be long.
Okay.
BANK
Hey, do you want to go grab a coffee?
My name's Andrew, by the way.

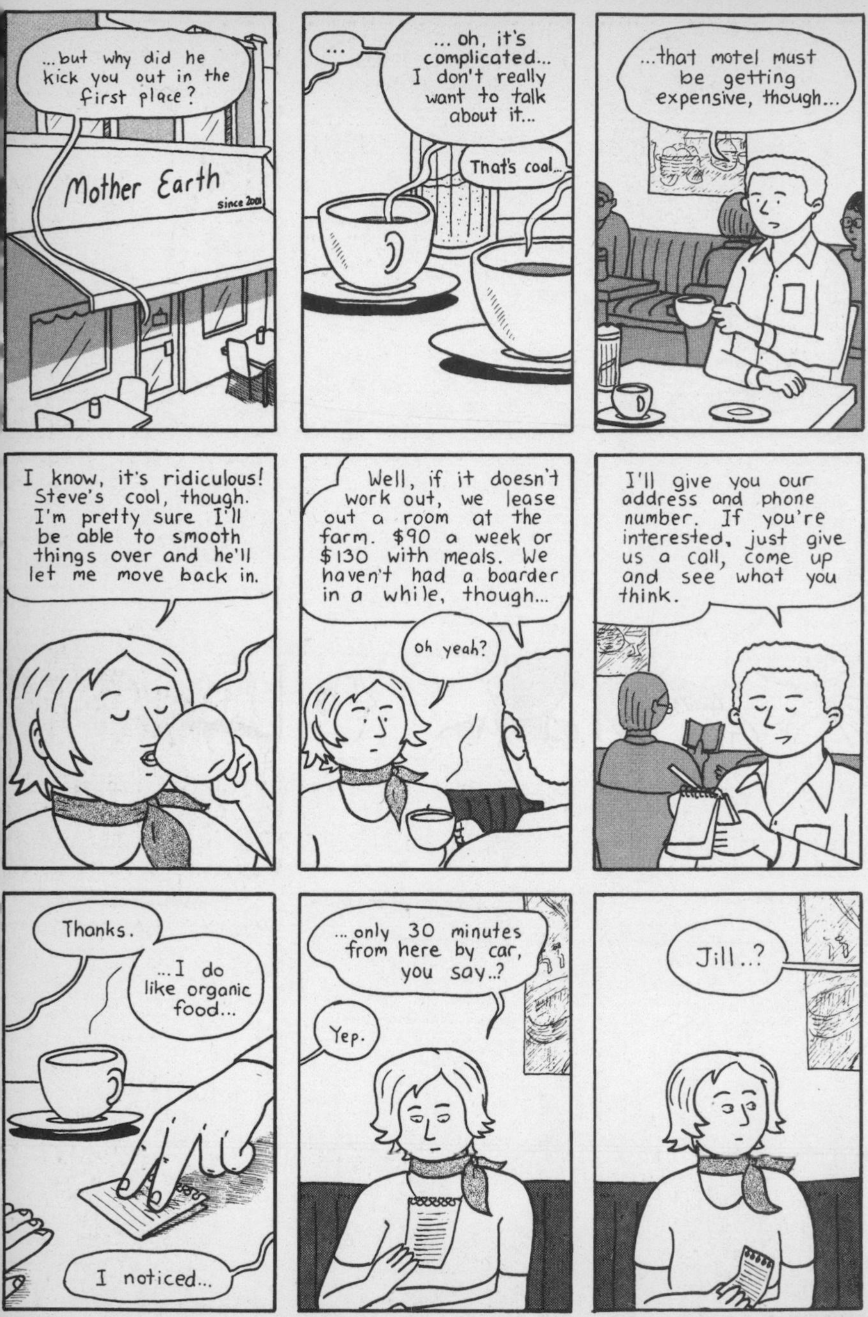
...but why did he kick you out in the first place?
Mother Earth
since 2001
...
... oh, it's complicated... I don't really want to talk about it...
That's cool...
...that motel must be getting expensive, though...
I know, it's ridiculous! Steve's cool, though. I'm pretty sure I'll be able to smooth things over and he'll let me move back in.
Well, if it doesn't work out, we lease out a room at the farm. $90 a week or $130 with meals. We haven't had a boarder in a while, though...
Oh yeah?
I'll give you our address and phone number. If you're interested, just give us a call, come up and see what you think.
Thanks.
...I do like organic food...
I noticed...
...only 30 minutes from here by car, you say..?
Yep.
Jill...?

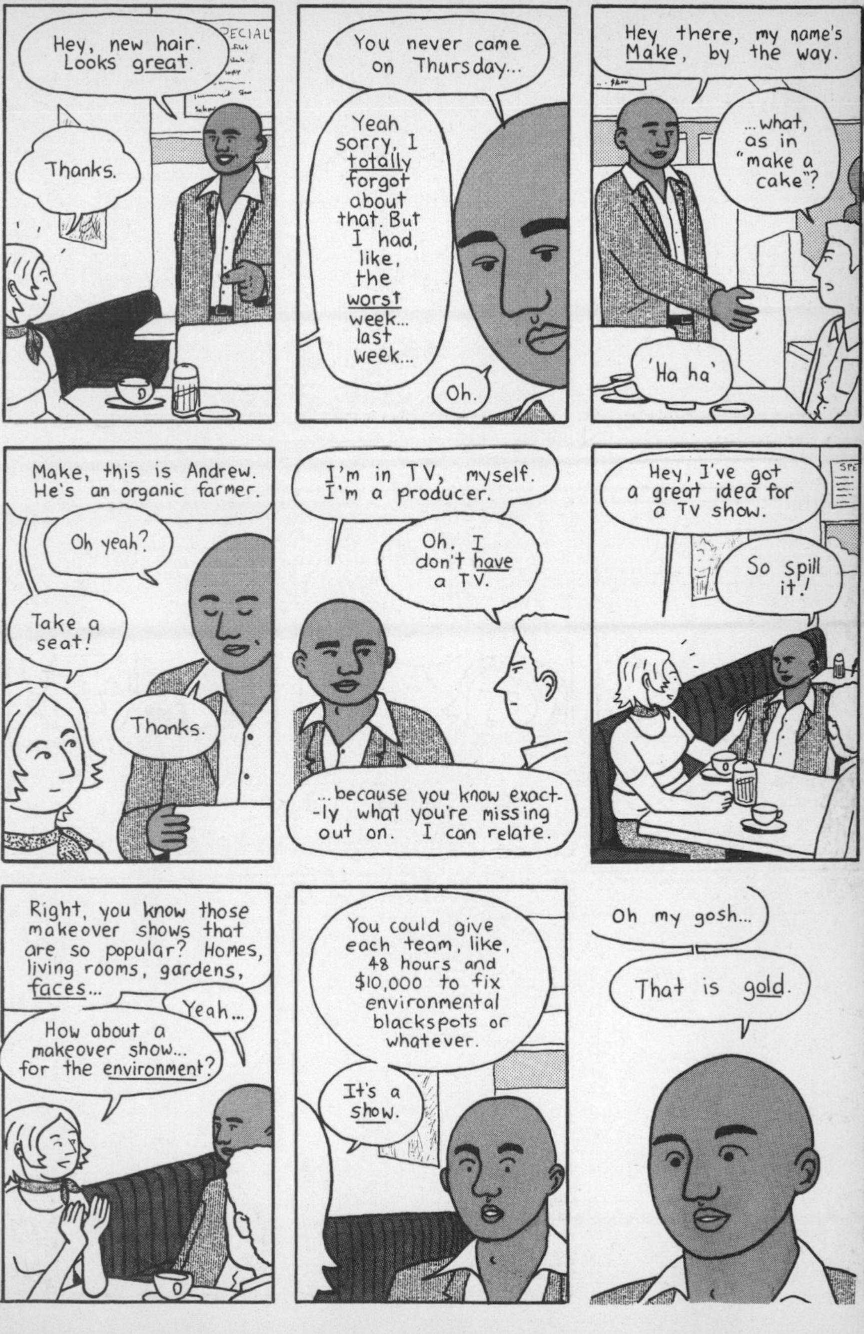
Hey, new hair. Looks great.
Thanks.
You never came on Thursday...
Yeah sorry, I totally forgot about that. But I had, like, the worst week... last week...
Oh.
Hey there, my name's Make, by the way.
...what, as in "make a cake"?
'Ha ha'
Make, this is Andrew. He's an organic farmer.
Oh yeah?
Take a seat!
Thanks.
I'm in TV, myself. I'm a producer.
Oh. I don't have a TV.
...because you know exact-ly what you're missing out on. I can relate.
Hey, I've got a great idea for a TV show.
So spill it!
Right, you know those makeover shows that are so popular? Homes, living rooms, gardens, faces...
Yeah...
How about a makeover show... for the environment?
You could give each team, like, 48 hours and $10,000 to fix environmental blackspots or whatever.
It's a show.
Oh my gosh...
That is gold.

Do you know why the environment is so boring? Because there's no drama!

You *just* solved that problem!

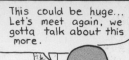

This could be huge... Let's meet again, we gotta talk about this more.

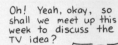

Give me your phone number, Jill.

Okay.

Right, I've got to get going. Steve's bound to be home watching car racing on TV right now, so I should catch him.

save!

Who's *Steve*?

Her boyfriend.

Oh! Yeah, okay, so shall we meet up this week to discuss the TV idea?

There's $2.50, Andrew.

Yeah! Sounds fun!

Catch you later!

Good luck!

Thanks!

tinkle tinkle

Do you *really* not have a TV, or did you just say that to impress her?

24

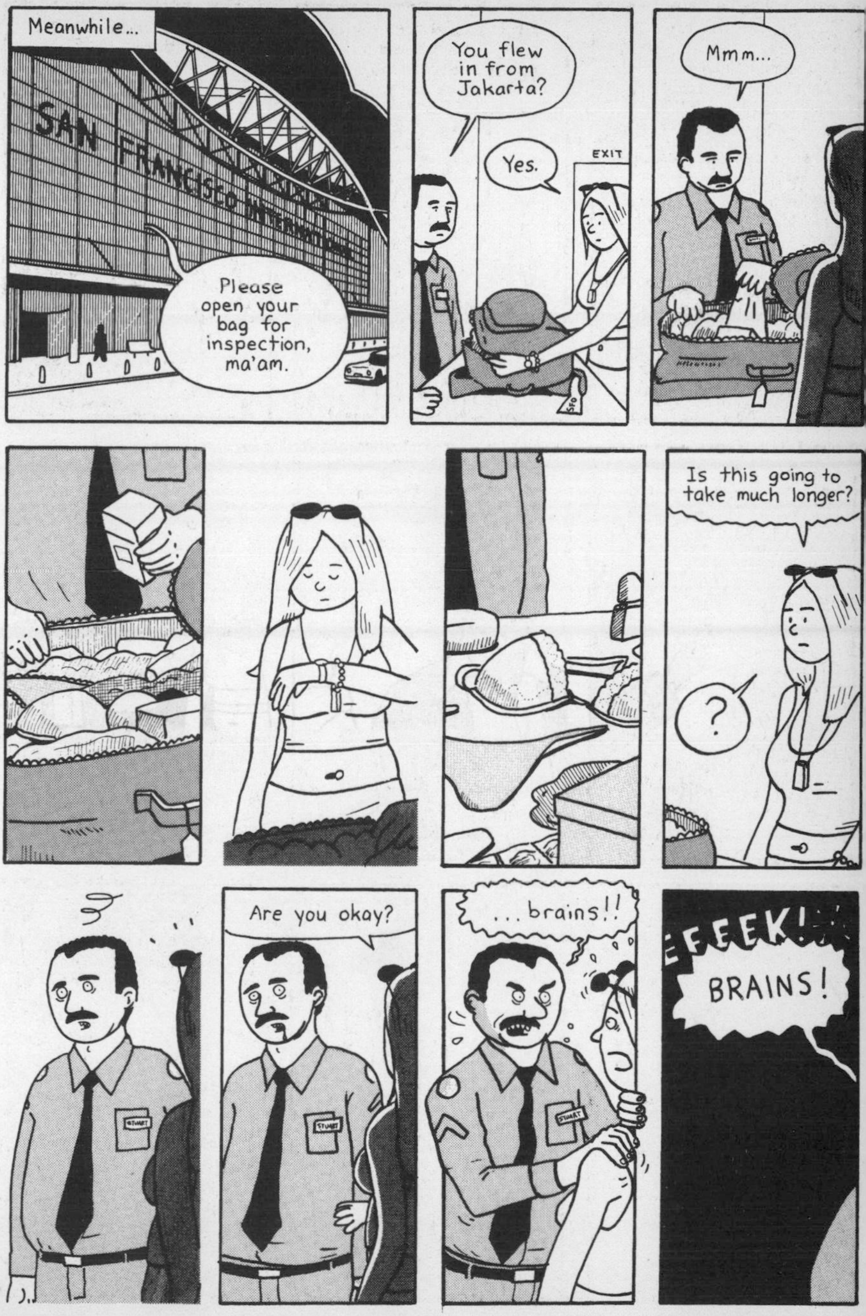
Meanwhile...
SAN FRANCISCO INTERNATIONAL
Please open your bag for inspection, ma'am.
You flew in from Jakarta?
Yes.
EXIT
Mmm...
Is this going to take much longer?
?
Are you okay?
...brains!!
EEEEK!
BRAINS!

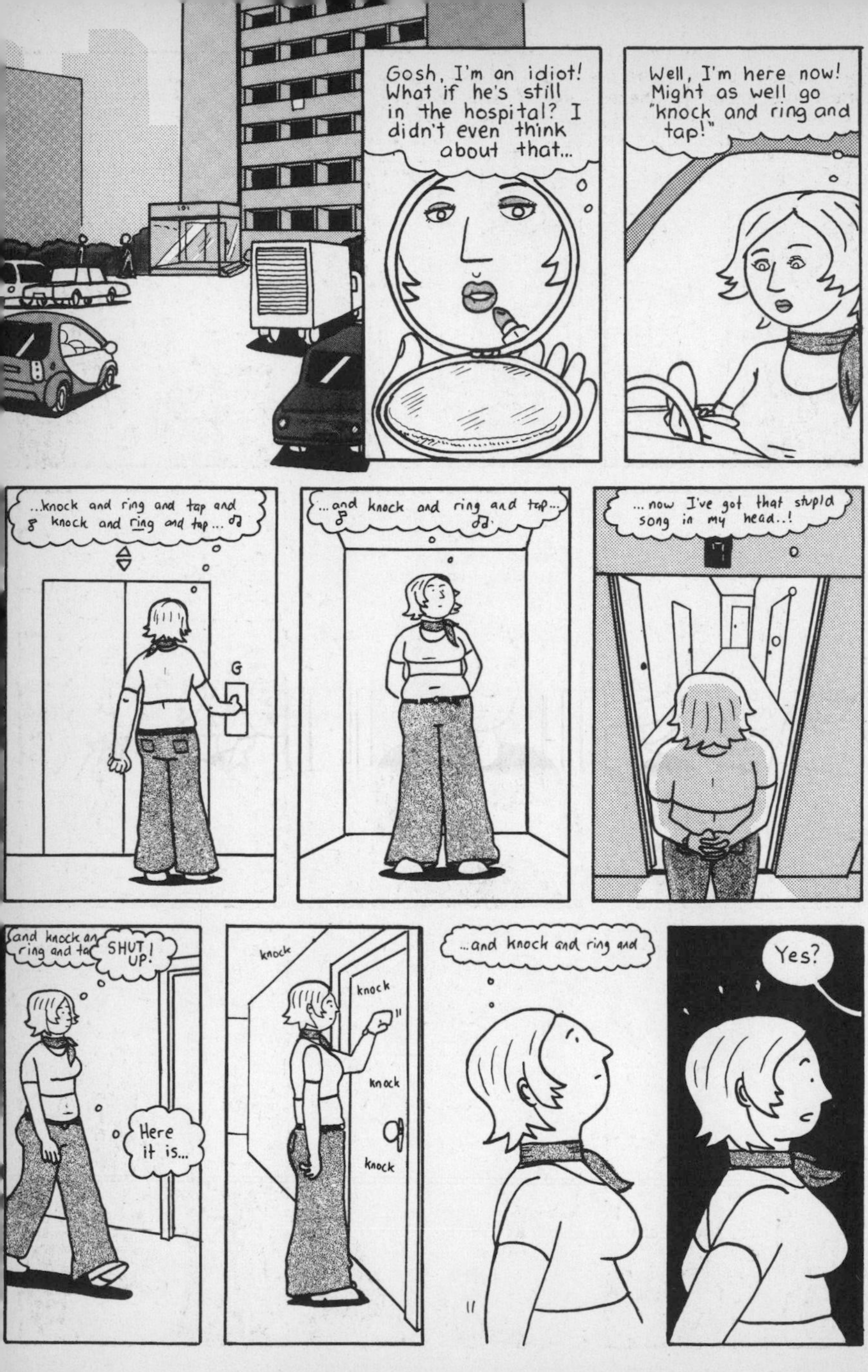

Gosh, I'm an idiot! What if he's still in the hospital? I didn't even think about that...
Well, I'm here now! Might as well go "knock and ring and tap!"
...knock and ring and tap and knock and ring and tap...
G
...and knock and ring and tap...
...now I've got that stupid song in my head..!
and knock and ring and ta
SHUT UP!
Here it is...
knock
knock
knock
knock
...and knock and ring and
Yes?

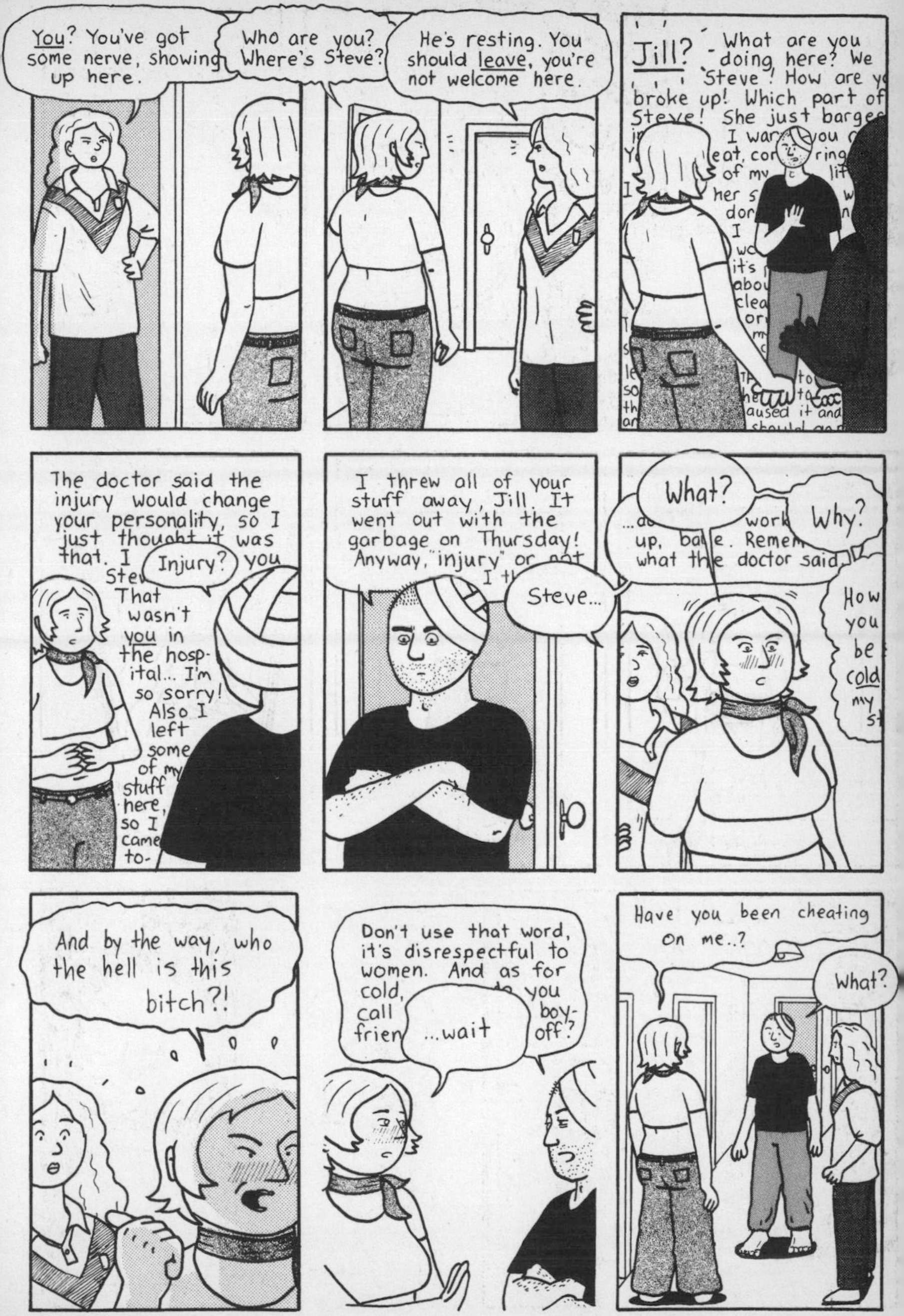
You? You've got some nerve, showing up here.
Who are you? Where's Steve?
He's resting. You should leave, you're not welcome here.
Jill?
What are you doing here? We broke up! Which part of
Steve! How are y
Steve! She just barge
The doctor said the injury would change your personality, so I just thought it was that. I
you
Injury?
That wasn't you in the hospital... I'm so sorry! Also I left some of my stuff here, so I came to-
I threw all of your stuff away, Jill. It went out with the garbage on Thursday! Anyway, "injury" or not
Steve...
What?
Why?
...do work up, babe. Remem what the doctor said.
How you be cold my
And by the way, who the hell is this bitch?!
Don't use that word, it's disrespectful to women. And as for cold, you call boy-frien off?
...wait
Have you been cheating on me..?
What?

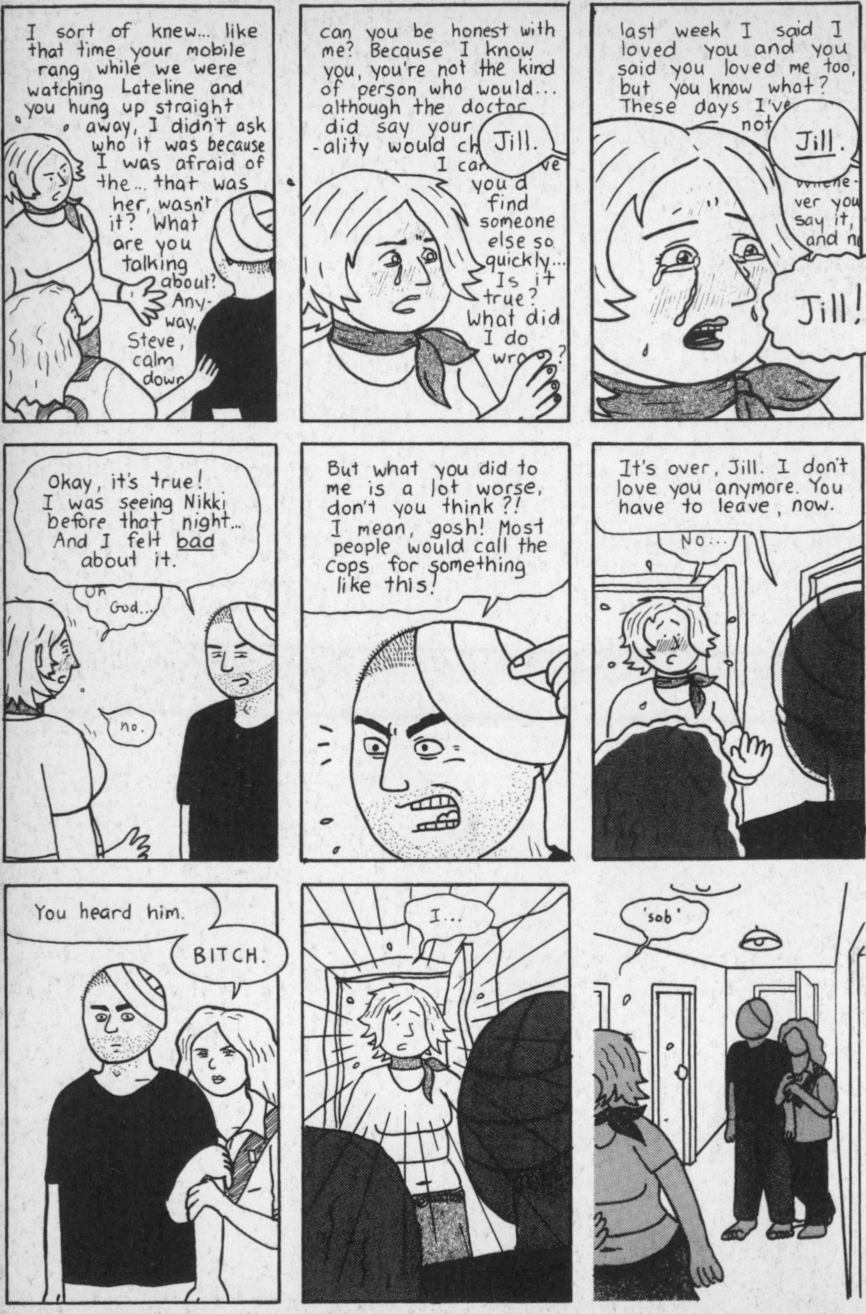

I sort of knew... like that time your mobile rang while we were watching Lateline and you hung up straight away, I didn't ask who it was because I was afraid of the... that was her, wasn't it?
What are you talking about? Any-way, Steve, calm down
can you be honest with me? Because I know you, you're not the kind of person who would... although the doctor did say your -ality would ch
Jill.
I can ve you'd find someone else so quickly... Is it true? What did I do wro ?
last week I said I loved you and you said you loved me too, but you know what? These days I've not
Jill.
whene-ver you say it, and n
Jill!
Okay, it's true! I was seeing Nikki before that night... And I felt bad about it.
Oh God...
no.
But what you did to me is a lot worse, don't you think?! I mean, gosh! Most people would call the cops for something like this!
It's over, Jill. I don't love you anymore. You have to leave, now.
No...
You heard him.
BITCH.
I...
'sob'

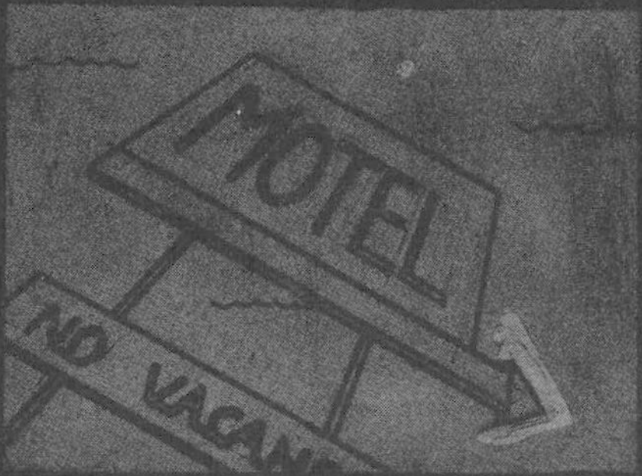
MOTEL

Chapter 2

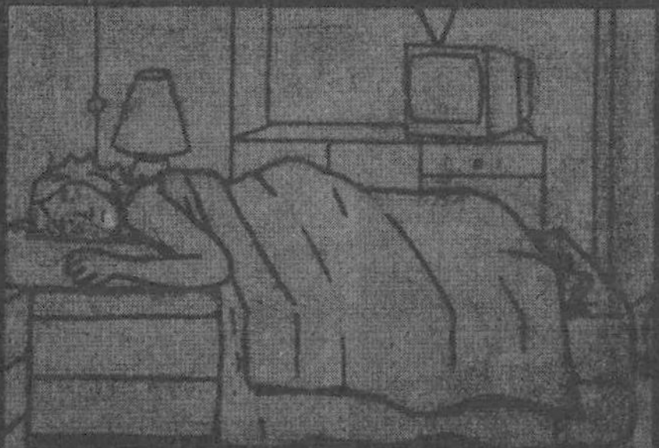

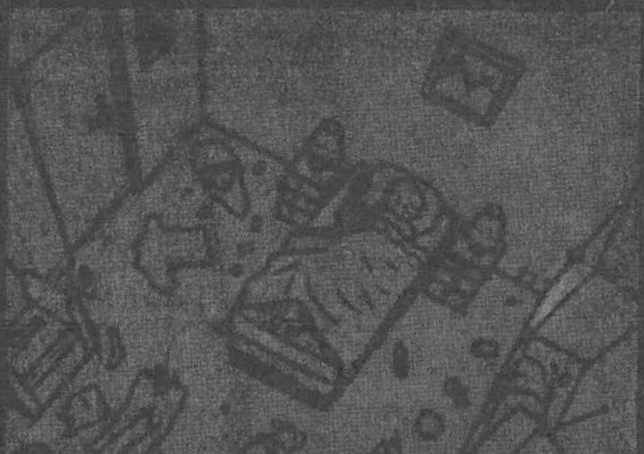

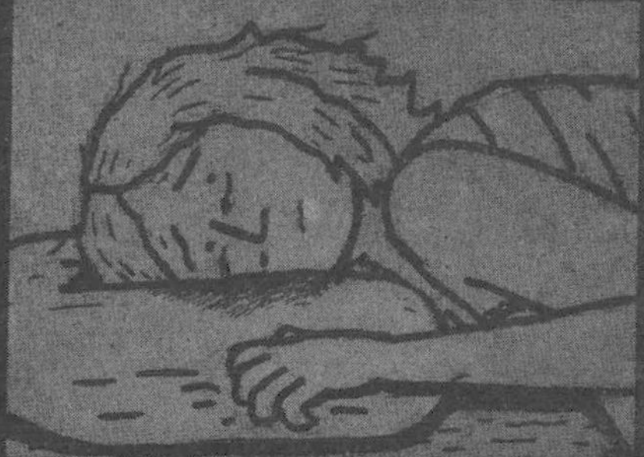

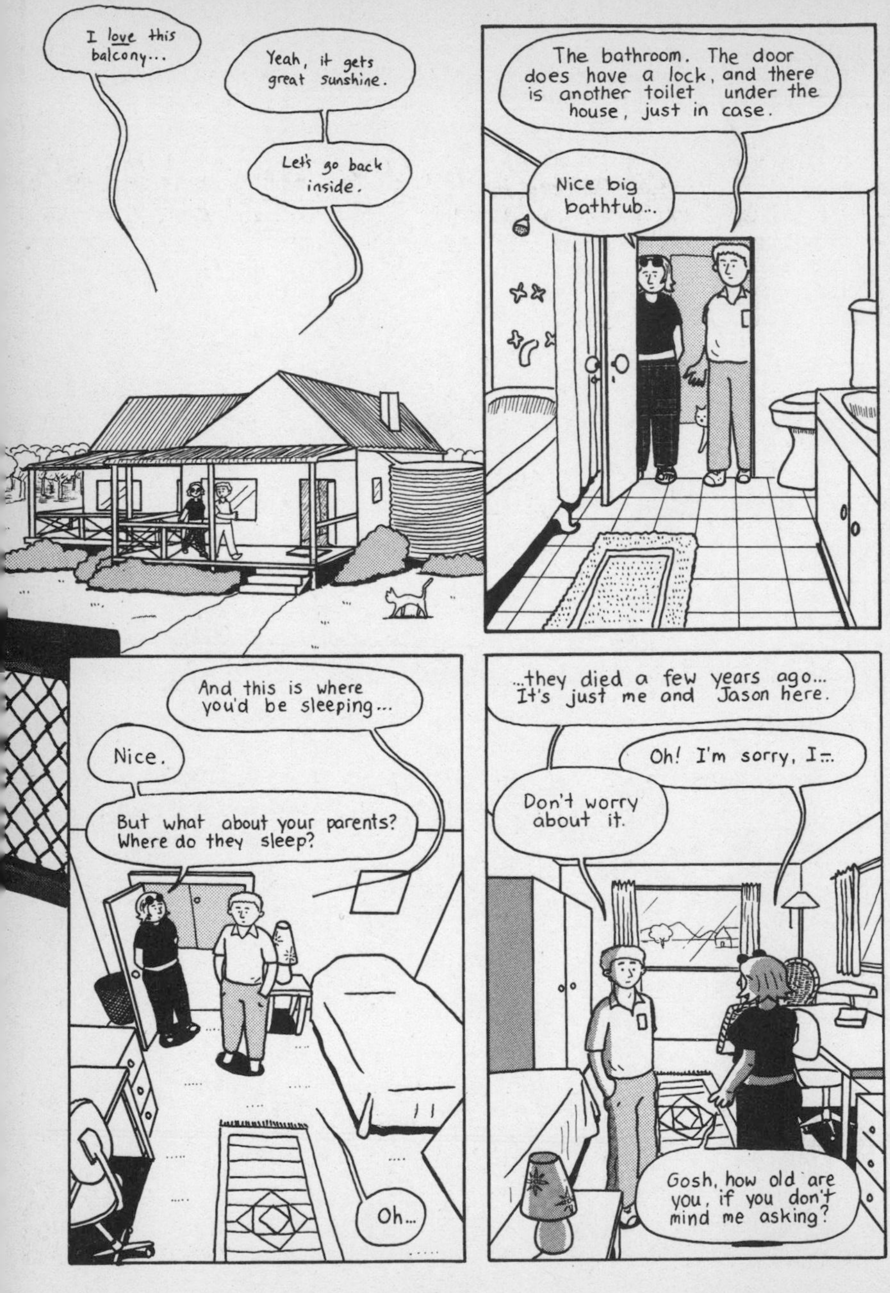

I love this balcony...
Yeah, it gets great sunshine.
Let's go back inside.
The bathroom. The door does have a lock, and there is another toilet under the house, just in case.
Nice big bathtub...
And this is where you'd be sleeping...
Nice.
But what about your parents? Where do they sleep?
Oh...
...they died a few years ago... It's just me and Jason here.
Oh! I'm sorry, I...
Don't worry about it.
Gosh, how old are you, if you don't mind me asking?

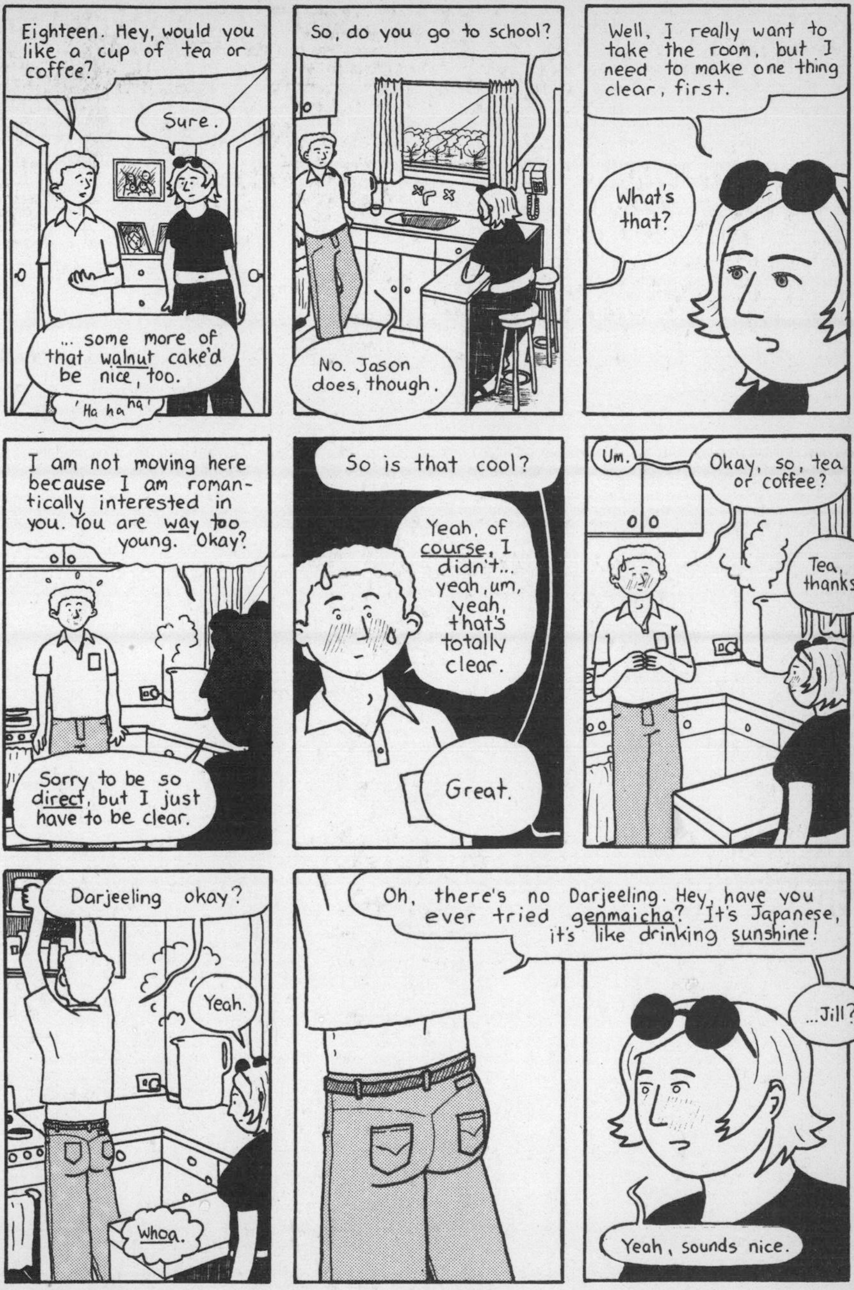
Eighteen. Hey, would you like a cup of tea or coffee?
Sure.
... some more of that walnut cake'd be nice, too.
'Ha ha ha'
So, do you go to school?
No. Jason does, though.
Well, I really want to take the room, but I need to make one thing clear, first.
What's that?
I am not moving here because I am romantically interested in you. You are way too young. Okay?
Sorry to be so direct, but I just have to be clear.
So is that cool?
Yeah, of course, I didn't... yeah, um, yeah, that's totally clear.
Great.
Um.
Okay, so, tea or coffee?
Tea, thanks.
Darjeeling okay?
Yeah.
Whoa.
Oh, there's no Darjeeling. Hey, have you ever tried genmaicha? It's Japanese, it's like drinking sunshine!
...Jill?
Yeah, sounds nice.

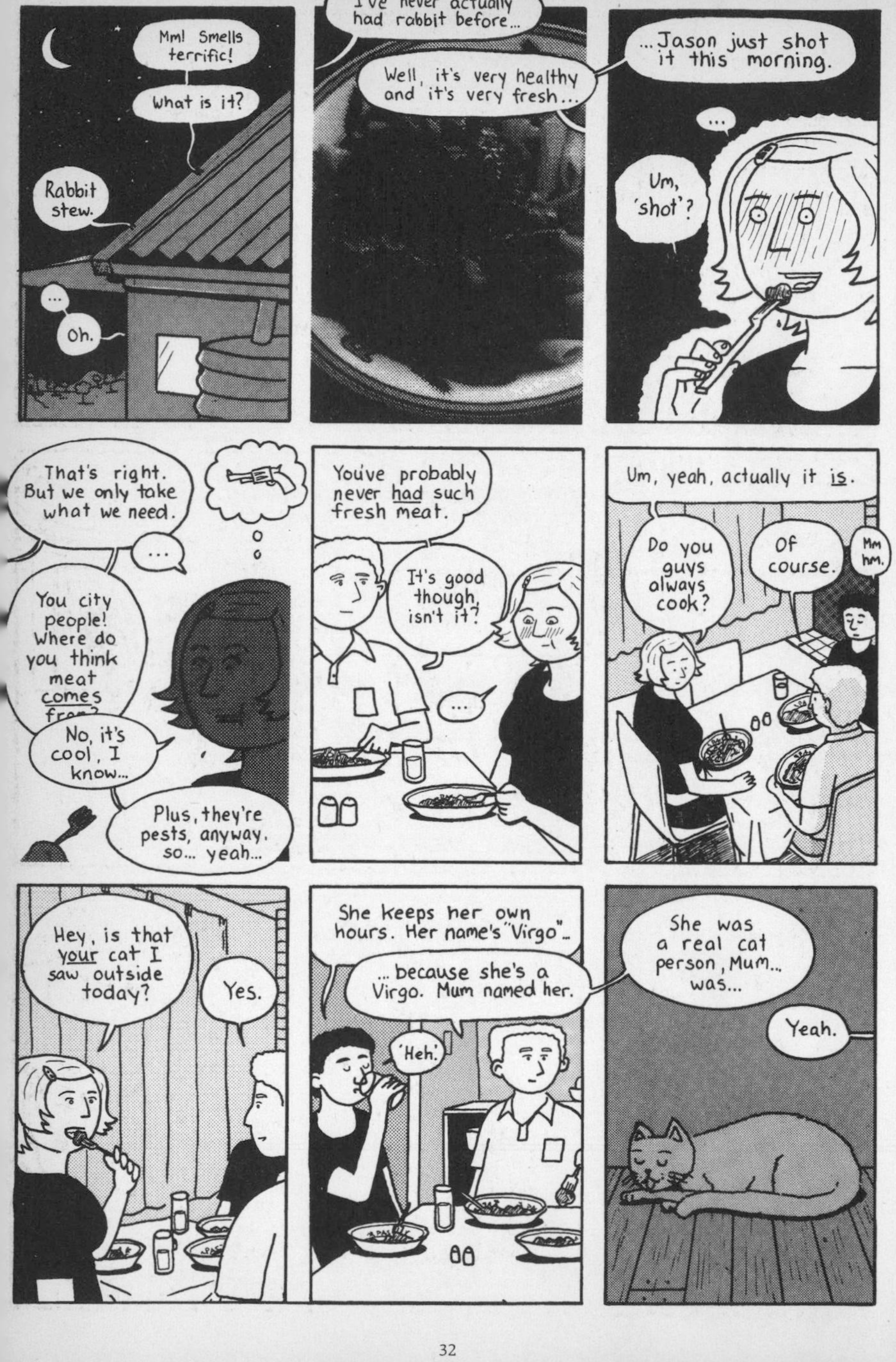

Mm! Smells terrific!
What is it?
Rabbit stew.
...
Oh.
I've never actually had rabbit before...
Well, it's very healthy and it's very fresh...
...Jason just shot it this morning.
...
Um, 'shot'?
That's right. But we only take what we need.
...
You city people! Where do you think meat comes
No, it's cool, I know...
Plus, they're pests, anyway. so... yeah...
You've probably never had such fresh meat.
It's good though, isn't it?
...
Um, yeah, actually it is.
Do you guys always cook?
Of course.
Mm hm.
Hey, is that your cat I saw outside today?
Yes.
She keeps her own hours. Her name's "Virgo"...
... because she's a Virgo. Mum named her.
'Heh.'
She was a real cat person, Mum... was...
Yeah.

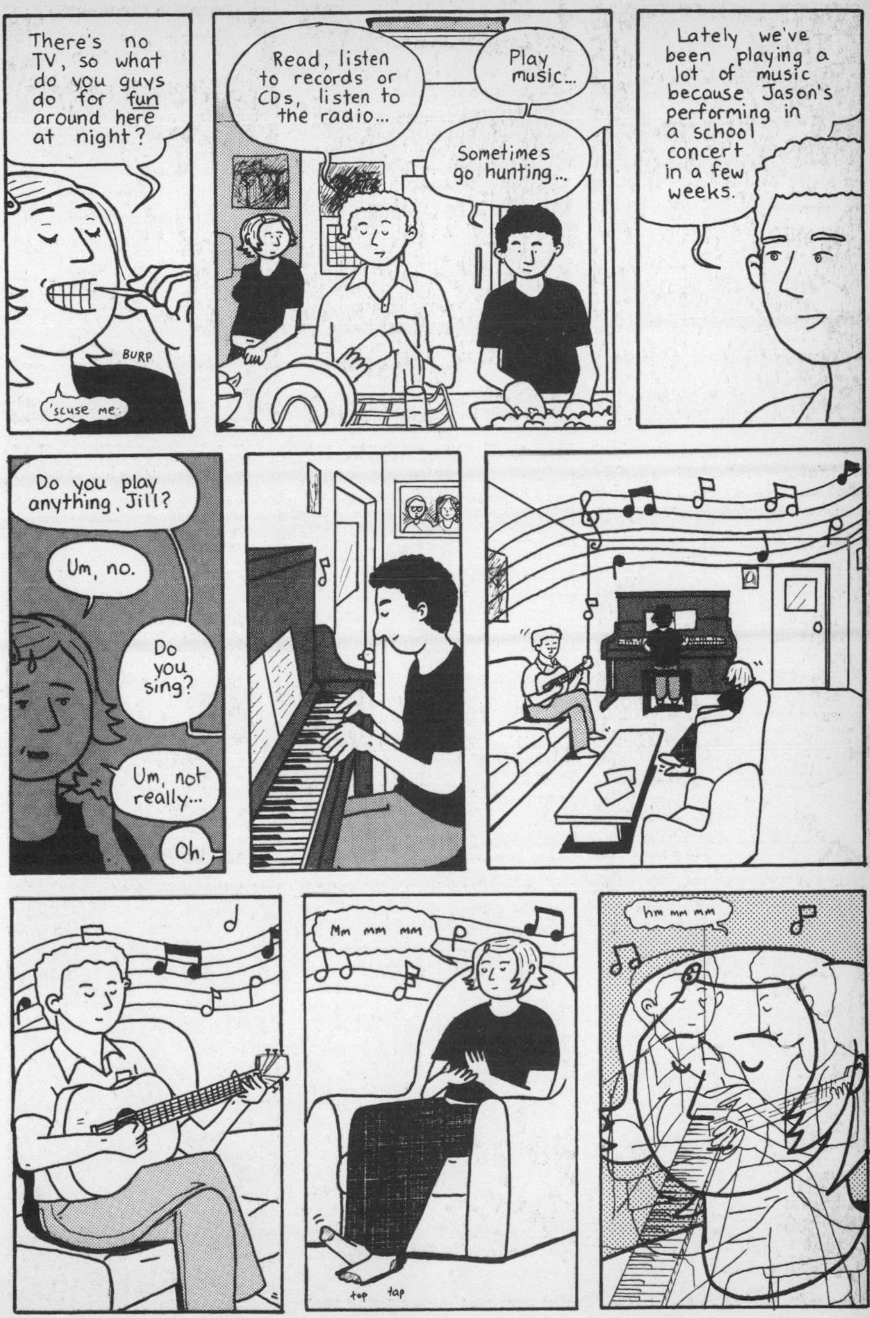
There's no TV, so what do you guys do for fun around here at night?
BURP
'scuse me.
Read, listen to records or CDs, listen to the radio...
Play music...
Sometimes go hunting...
Lately we've been playing a lot of music because Jason's performing in a school concert in a few weeks.
Do you play anything, Jill?
Um, no.
Do you sing?
Um, not really...
Oh.
Mm mm mm
tap tap
hm mm mm

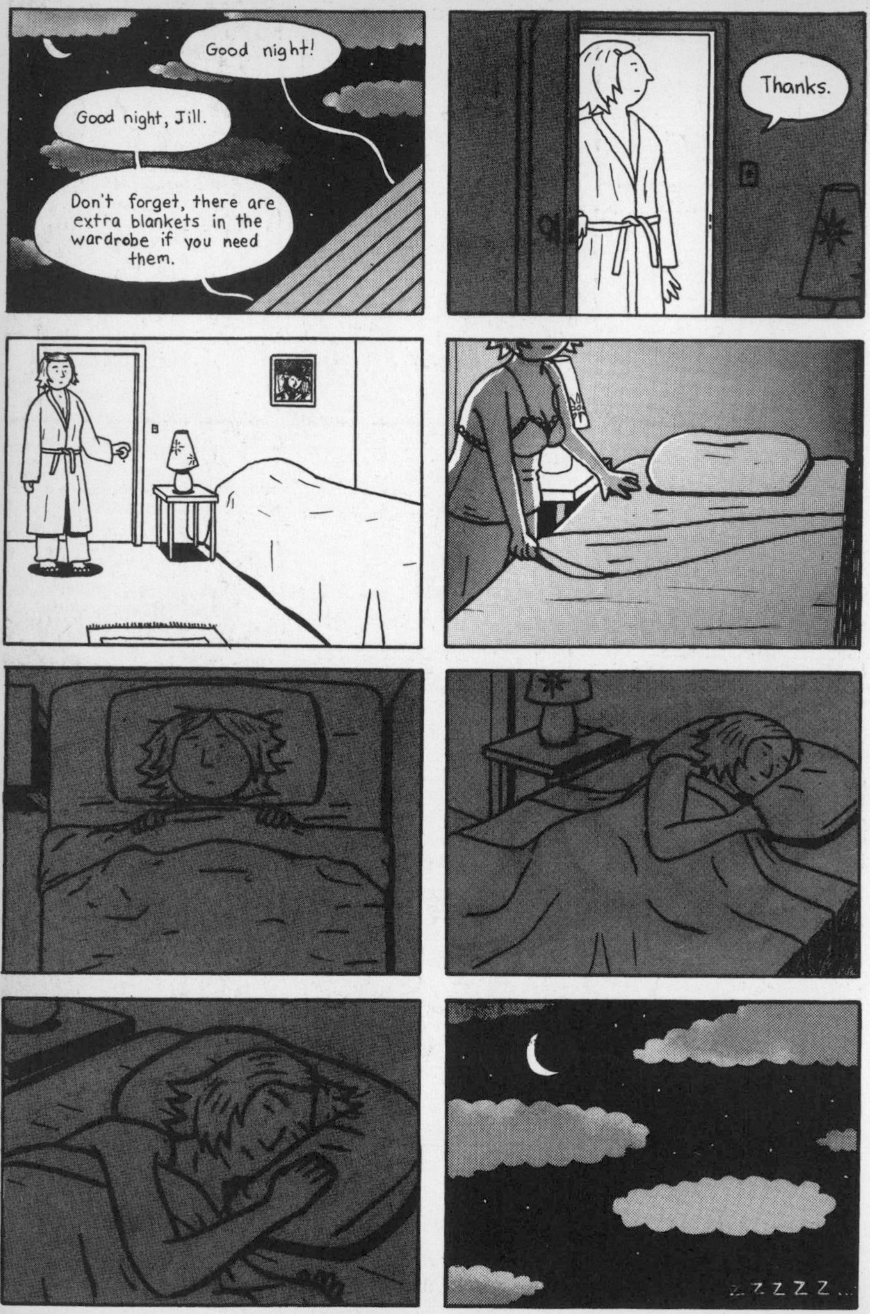
Good night!
Good night, Jill.
Don't forget, there are extra blankets in the wardrobe if you need them.
Thanks.
Z Z Z Z Z ...

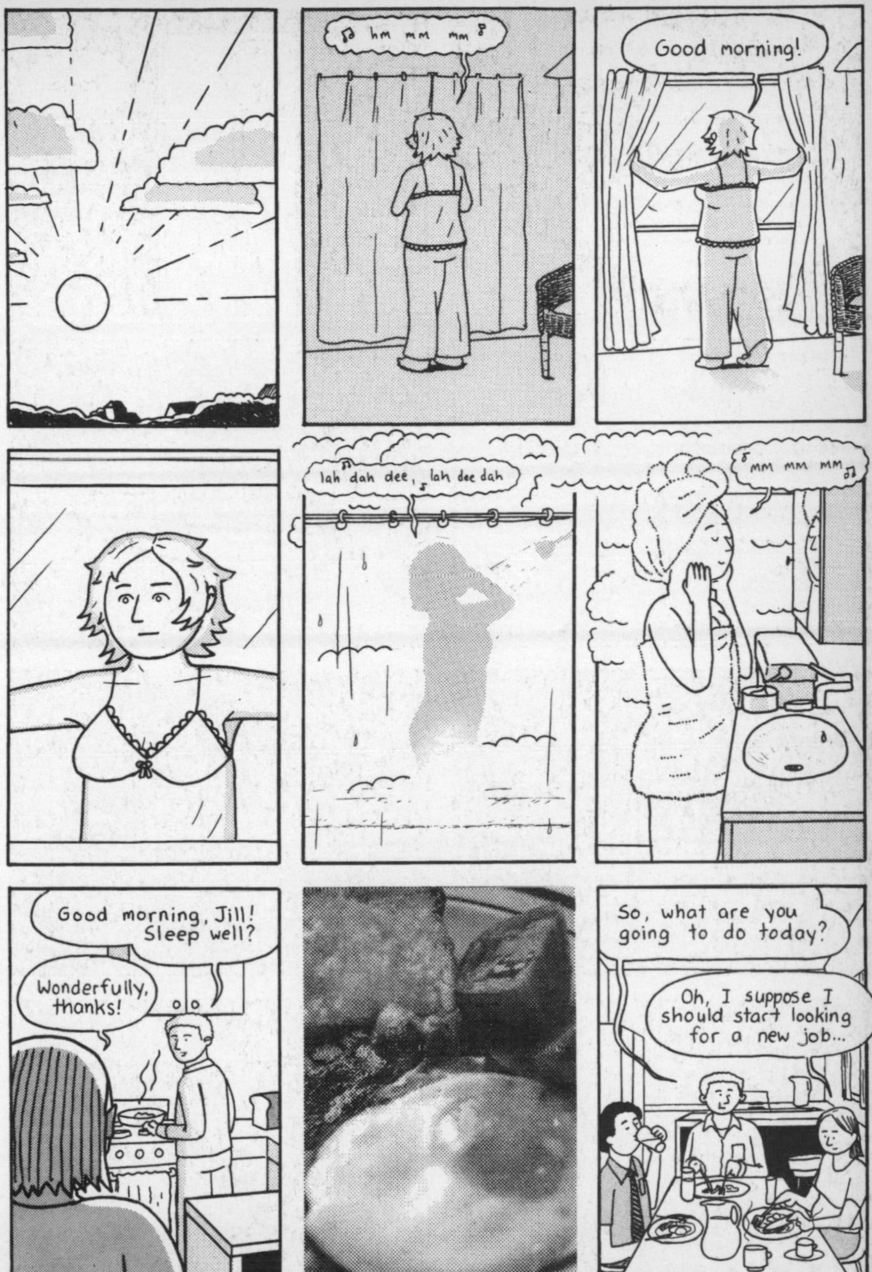
hm mm mm
Good morning!
lah dah dee, lah dee dah
mm mm mm
Good morning, Jill! Sleep well?
Wonderfully, thanks!
So, what are you going to do today?
Oh, I suppose I should start looking for a new job...

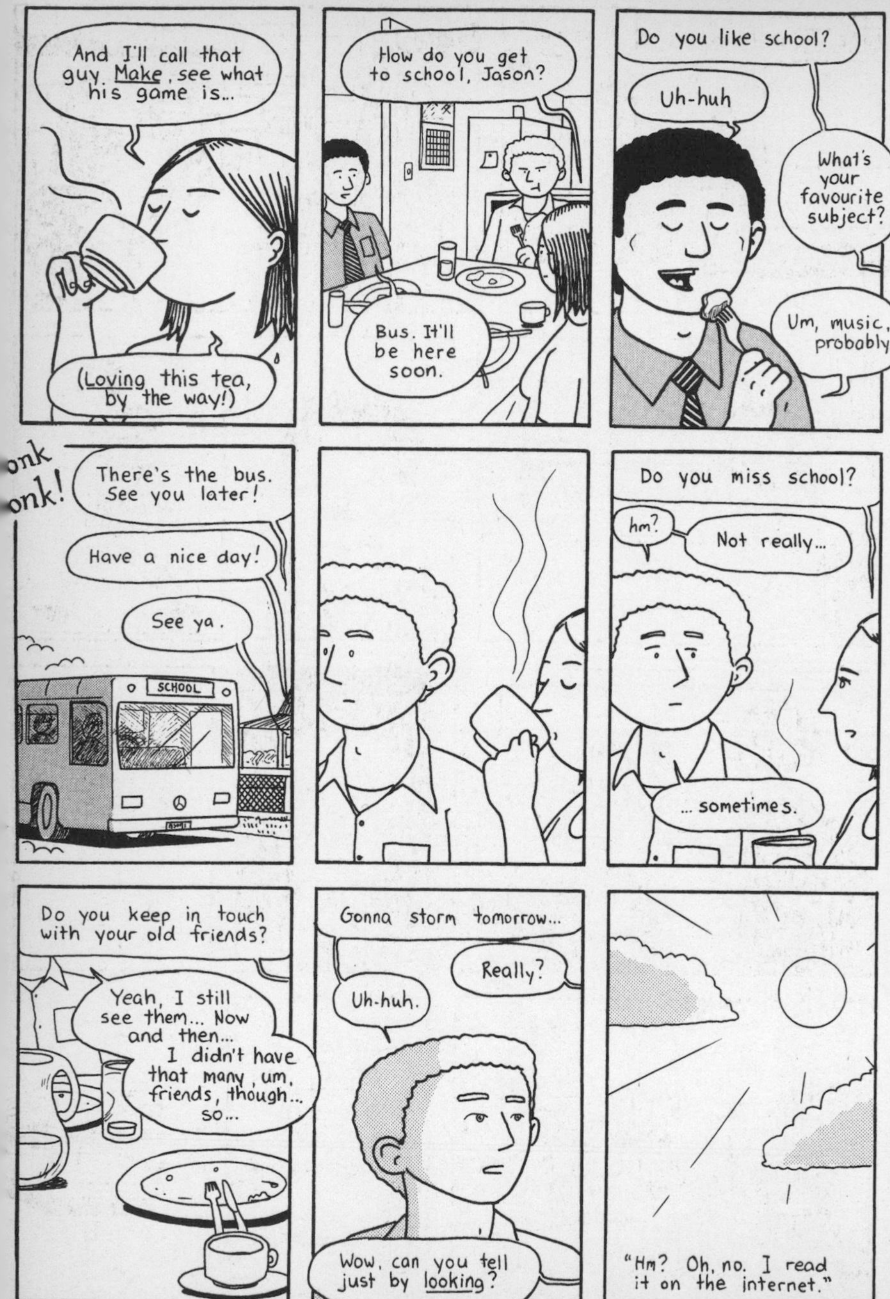
And I'll call that guy Make, see what his game is...
(Loving this tea, by the way!)
How do you get to school, Jason?
Bus. It'll be here soon.
Do you like school?
Uh-huh
What's your favourite subject?
Um, music, probably.
onk onk!
There's the bus. See you later!
Have a nice day!
See ya.
SCHOOL
Do you miss school?
hm?
Not really...
... sometimes.
Do you keep in touch with your old friends?
Yeah, I still see them... Now and then...
I didn't have that many, um, friends, though... so...
Gonna storm tomorrow...
Really?
Uh-huh.
Wow, can you tell just by looking?
"Hm? Oh, no. I read it on the internet."

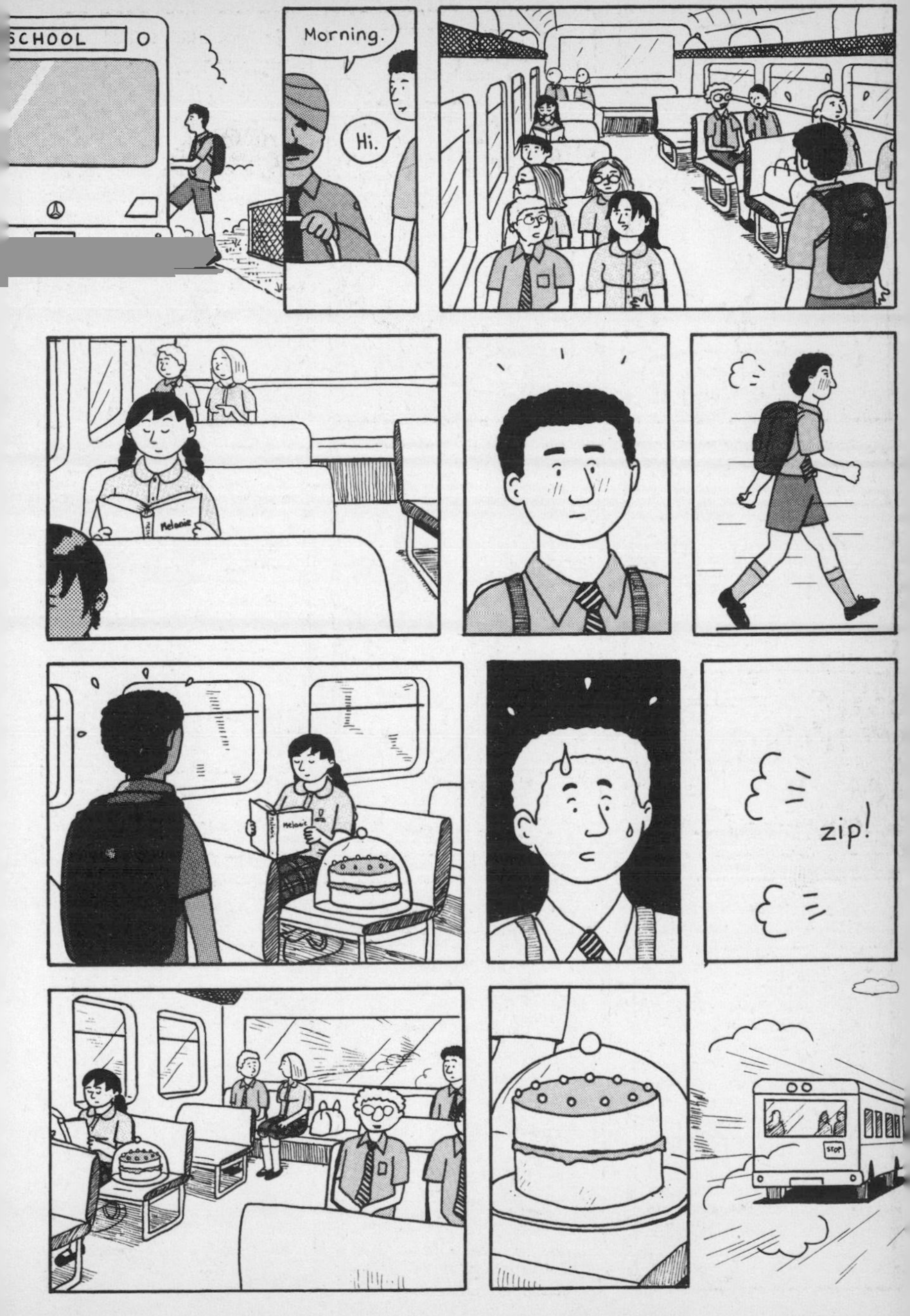
SCHOOL
Morning.
Hi.
Melanie
zip!

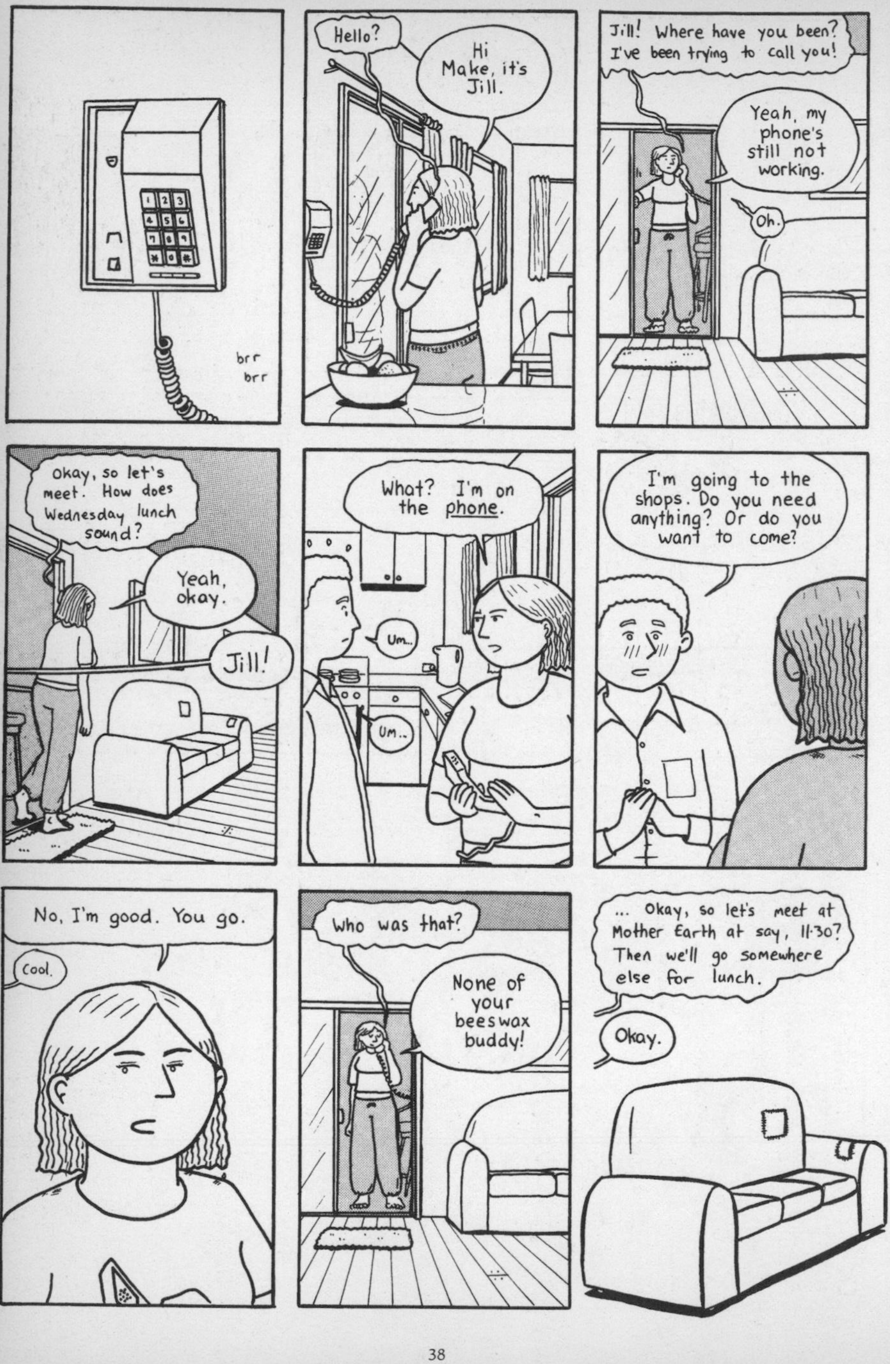

brr
brr
Hello?
Hi Make, it's Jill.
Jill! Where have you been? I've been trying to call you!
Yeah, my phone's still not working.
Oh.
Okay, so let's meet. How does Wednesday lunch sound?
Yeah, okay.
Jill!
What? I'm on the phone.
Um..
Um..
I'm going to the shops. Do you need anything? Or do you want to come?
No, I'm good. You go.
Cool.
Who was that?
None of your beeswax buddy!
... Okay, so let's meet at Mother Earth at say, 11·30? Then we'll go somewhere else for lunch.
Okay.

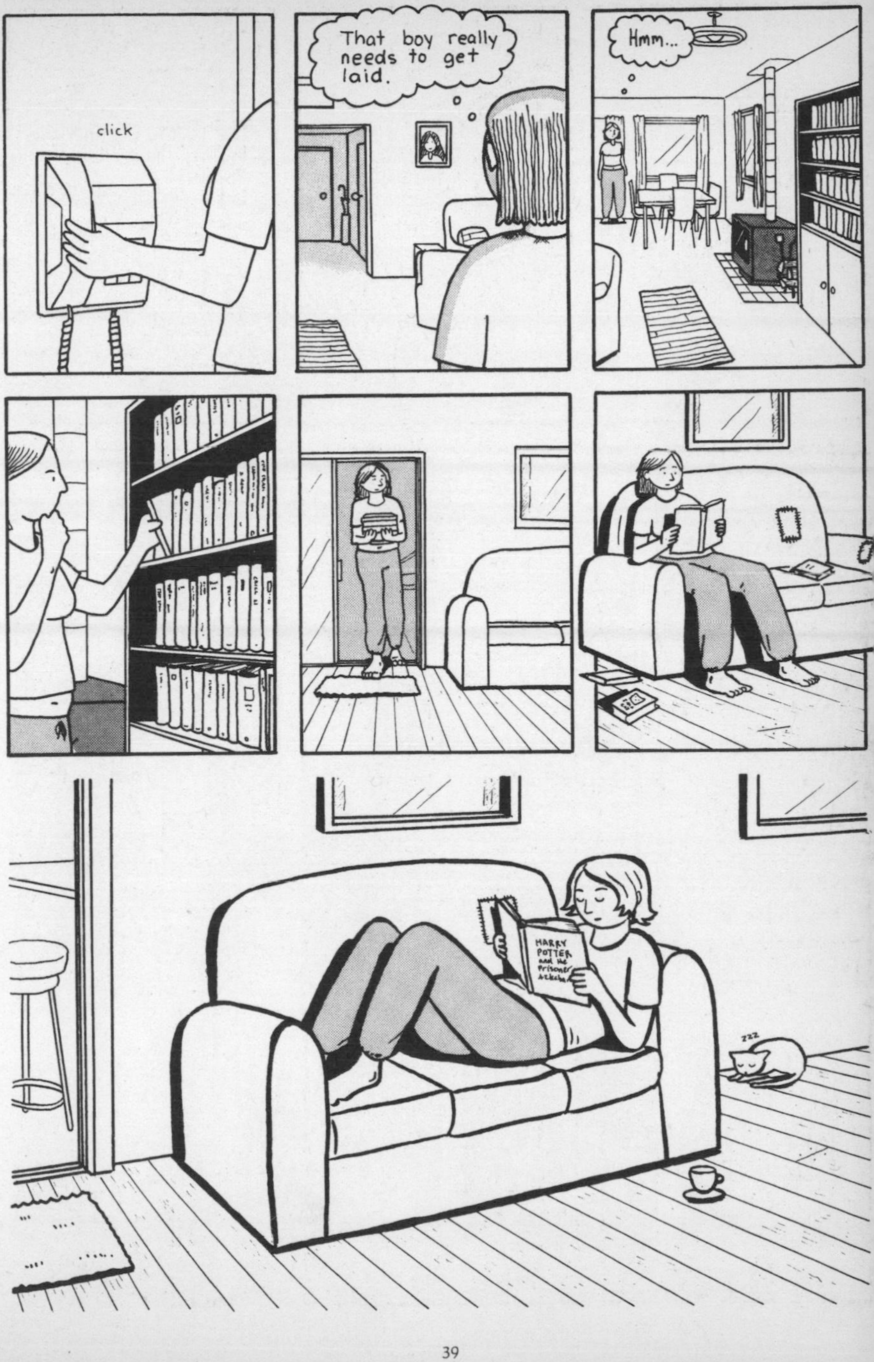
click
That boy really needs to get laid.
Hmm...
HARRY POTTER and the Prisoner of Azkaban
zzz

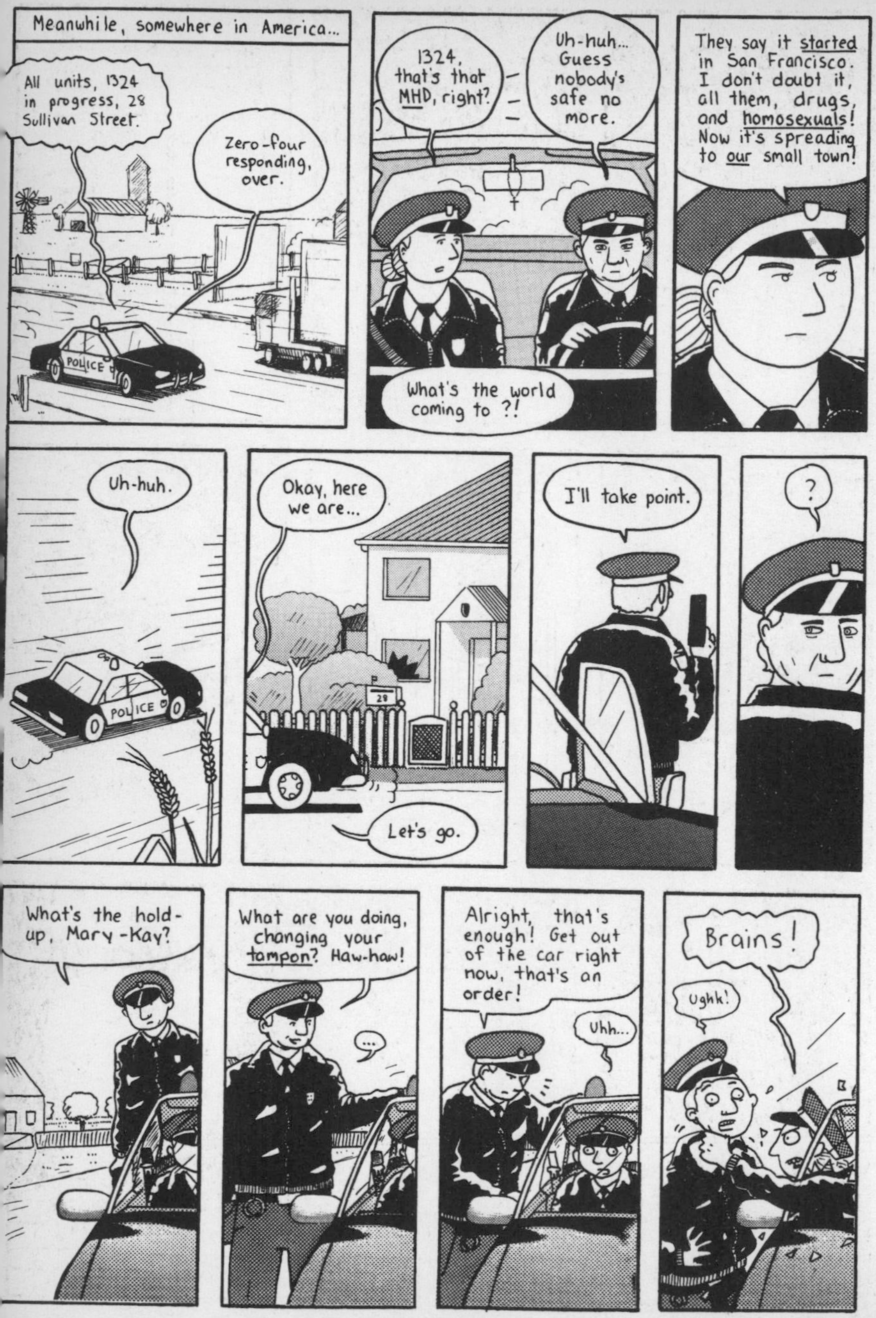
Meanwhile, somewhere in America...
All units, 1324 in progress, 28 Sullivan Street.
Zero-four responding, over.
1324, that's that MHD, right?
Uh-huh... Guess nobody's safe no more.
What's the world coming to ?!
They say it started in San Francisco. I don't doubt it, all them, drugs, and homosexuals! Now it's spreading to our small town!
Uh-huh.
Okay, here we are...
Let's go.
I'll take point.
?
What's the hold-up, Mary-Kay?
What are you doing, changing your tampon? Haw-haw!
...
Alright, that's enough! Get out of the car right now, that's an order!
Uhh...
Brains!
Ughk!

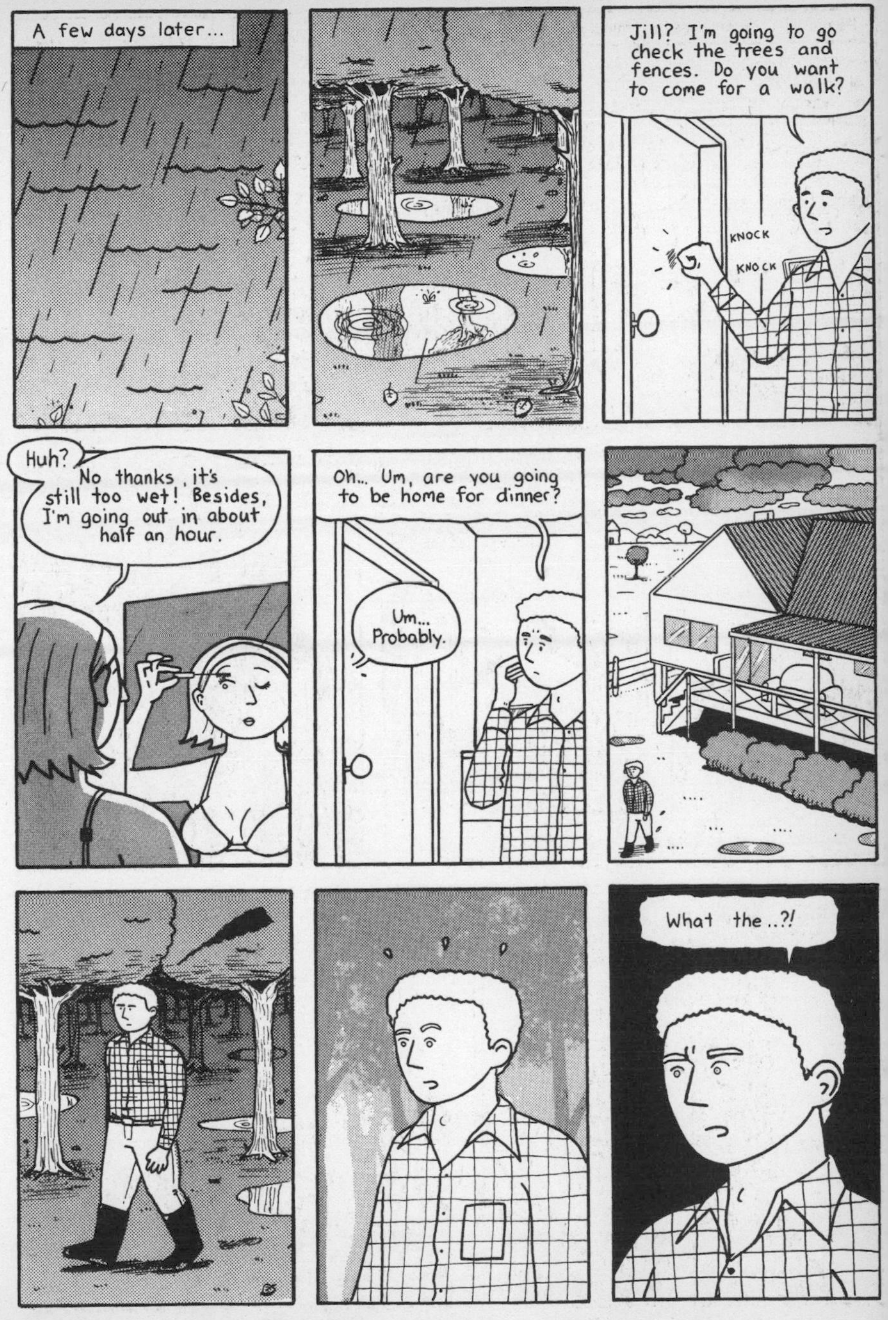
A few days later...
Jill? I'm going to go check the trees and fences. Do you want to come for a walk?
KNOCK
KNOCK
Huh?
No thanks, it's still too wet! Besides, I'm going out in about half an hour.
Oh... Um, are you going to be home for dinner?
Um... Probably.
What the..?!

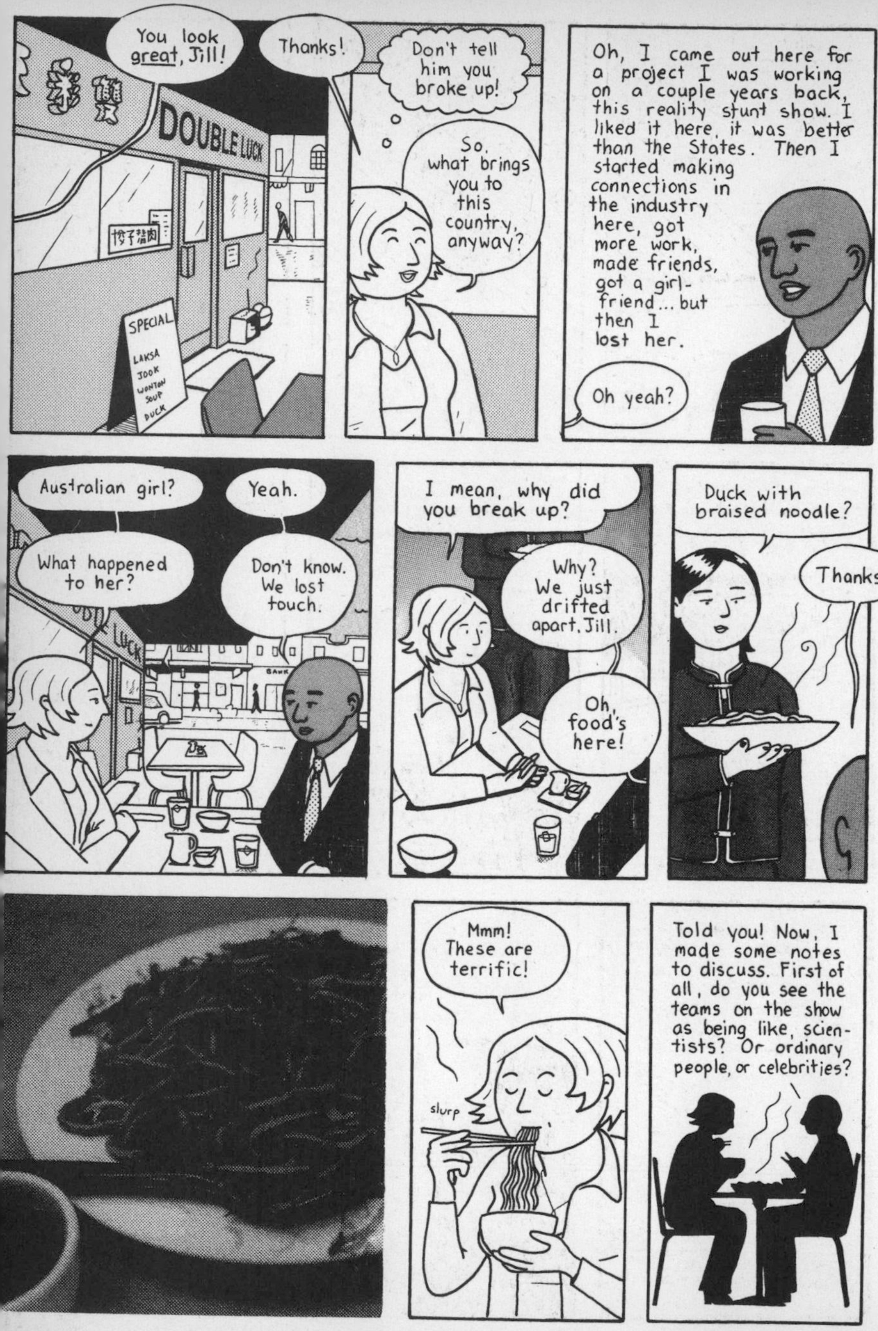
DOUBLE LUCK
You look great, Jill!
Thanks!
Don't tell him you broke up!
So, what brings you to this country, anyway?
SPECIAL
LAKSA
JOOK
WONTON SOUP
DUCK
Oh, I came out here for a project I was working on a couple years back, this reality stunt show. I liked it here, it was better than the States. Then I started making connections in the industry here, got more work, made friends, got a girl-friend... but then I lost her.
Oh yeah?
Australian girl?
Yeah.
What happened to her?
Don't know. We lost touch.
I mean, why did you break up?
Why? We just drifted apart, Jill.
Oh, food's here!
Duck with braised noodle?
Thanks.
Mmm! These are terrific!
slurp
Told you! Now, I made some notes to discuss. First of all, do you see the teams on the show as being like, scien-tists? Or ordinary people, or celebrities?

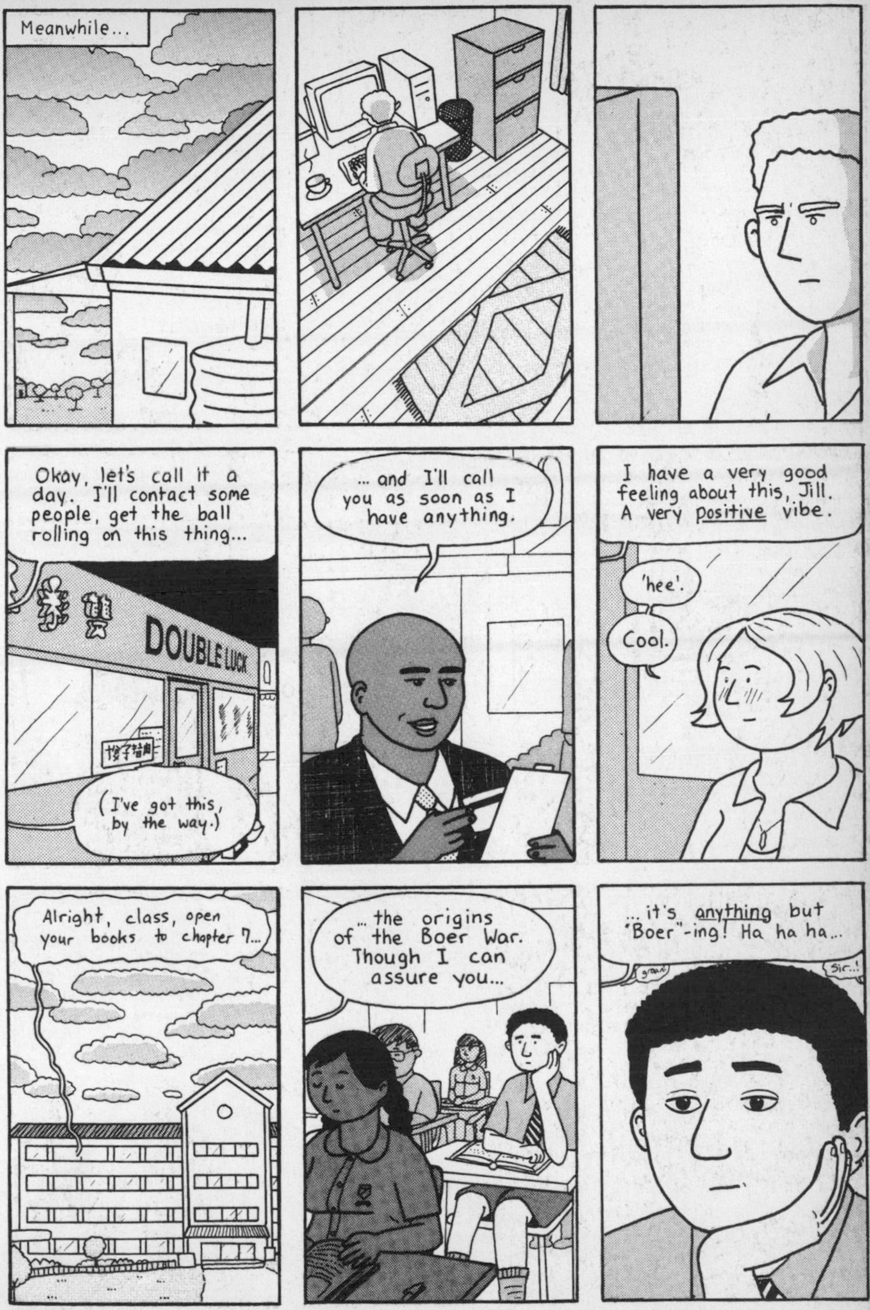
Meanwhile...
Okay, let's call it a day. I'll contact some people, get the ball rolling on this thing...
DOUBLE LUCK
(I've got this, by the way.)
... and I'll call you as soon as I have anything.
I have a very good feeling about this, Jill. A very positive vibe.
'hee'.
Cool.
Alright, class, open your books to chapter 7...
... the origins of the Boer War. Though I can assure you...
... it's anything but "Boer"-ing! Ha ha ha...
groan
Sir..!

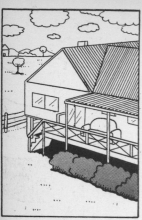

I'm back!

Hm.

Well.

I need *music*.

Let's see what you've got, Andy-boy!

Hmm... classical, jazz, classical, The White Album...

Hello, what's this?

TRIMP

" I have a very good feeling about this, Jill."

THERE'S A WRINKLE IN OUR TIME
(1984)

T R A M P

1984

" A very positive vibe..."

Mmm...

44

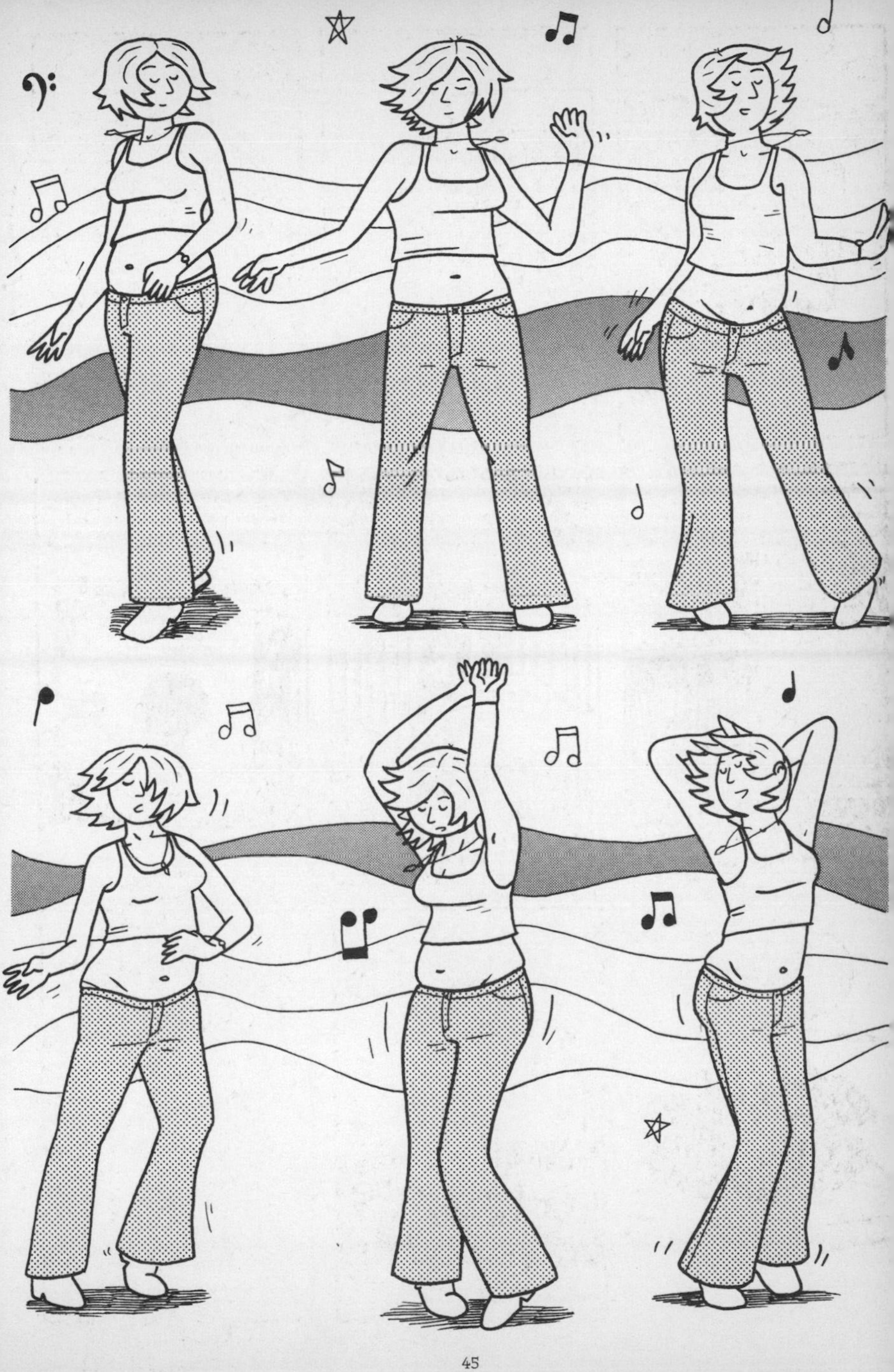

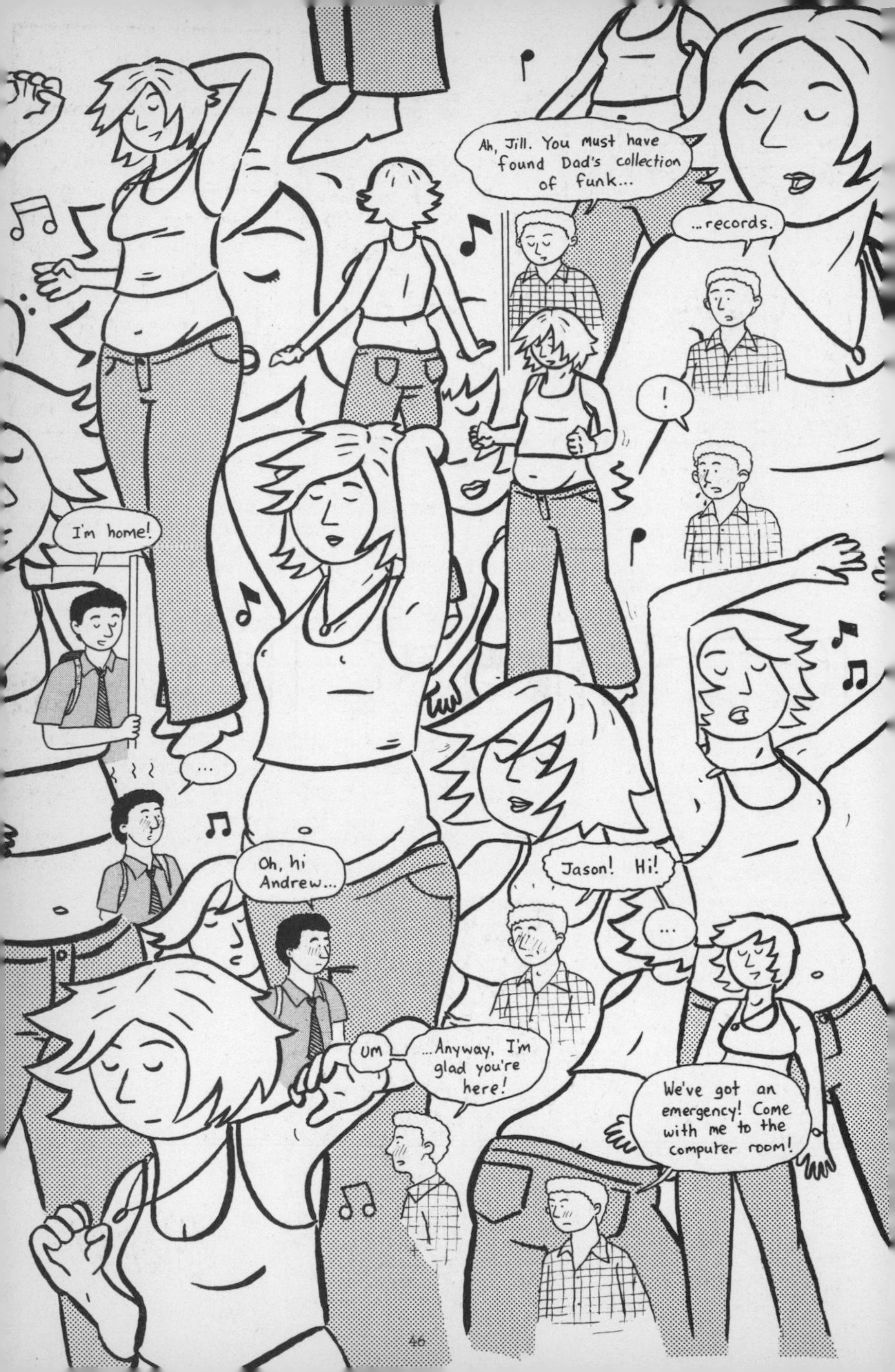

Ah, Jill. You must have found Dad's collection of funk...
...records.
!
I'm home!
...
Oh, hi Andrew...
Jason! Hi!
...
UM
...Anyway, I'm glad you're here!
We've got an emergency! Come with me to the computer room!

We've got a serious infestation of _these_ in the orchard.

Whoa.

They've already killed two trees. I didn't burn them because it's so wet out there today.

But, according to the research I did today, that may not be enough! These beetles are incredibly voracious, and have an extremely rapid breeding cycle.

These are no ordinary beetles.

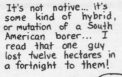

It's not native... it's some kind of hybrid, or mutation of a South American borer... I read that one guy lost twelve hectares in a fortnight to them!

Jeez.

What can we do?

Burn them out by hand, and keep looking to see if it has any natural enemies.

...there _is_ a poison... but guess who makes it?

Andoria?

Yep.

Huh.

They had a lot of information about the beetles on on their website, though...

Yeah, they _would._

Yeah.

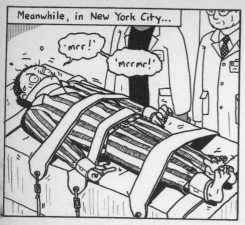

Meanwhile, in New York City...

'mrr!'

'mrrmr!'

Think they'll hold this time?

Hope so. They're military grade, so...

SANDRA MAZIWA

HIKARI HACHIMITSU

The question is, "Are we going to have enough this time next week?"

Is anyone?

Hm.

HOSPITAL

The government is really dragging on this.

- as usual.

...what an awful disease.

mmm...

If only we knew what caused it.

'ding'

Got another one, doctors.

mmnf!

She was on the subway when it happened. Three fatalities... The tranquilizer must have only grazed her - she was awake again like, ten minutes later.

'Mmn!'

'MMNF!'

'mnf!'

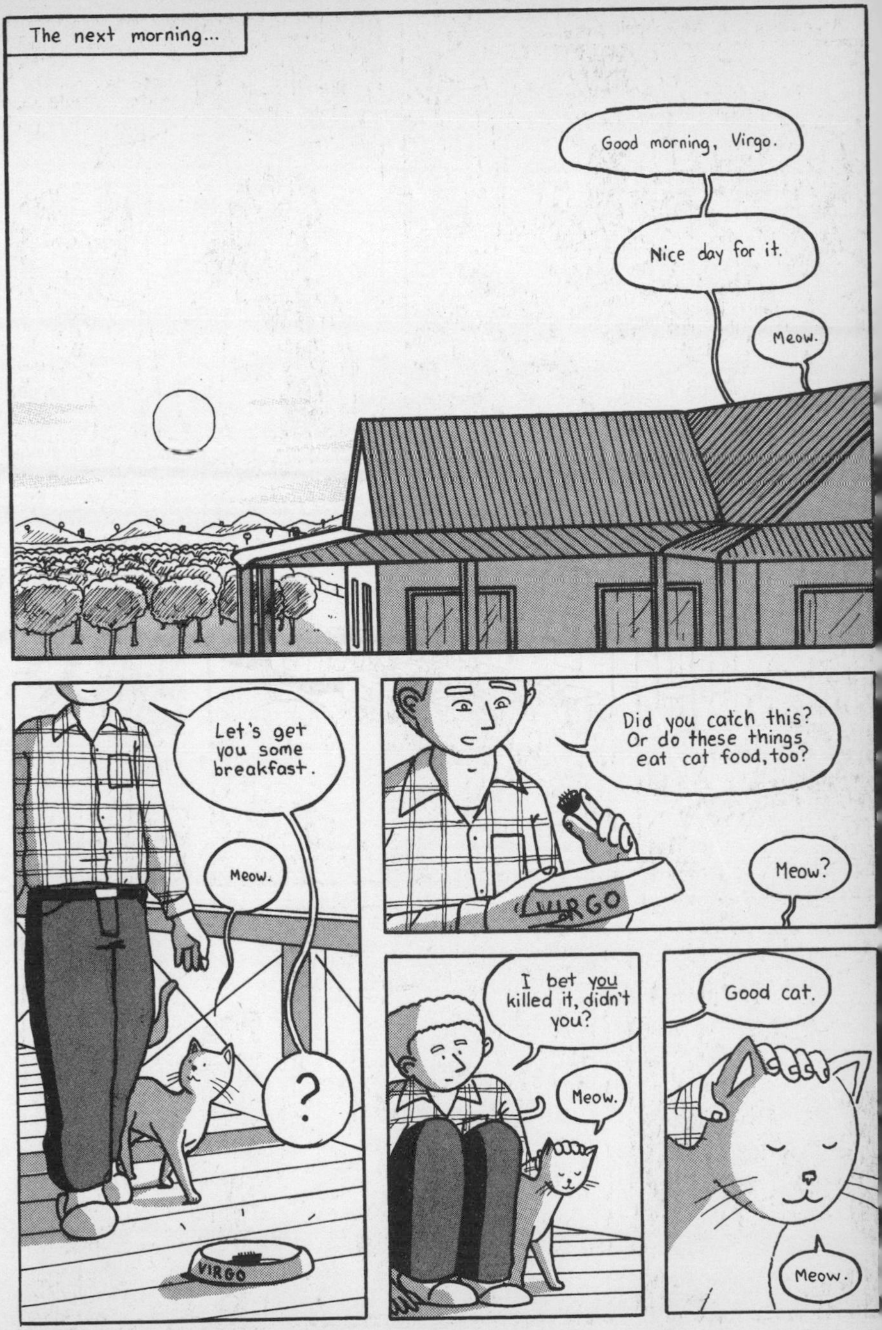
The next morning...
Good morning, Virgo.
Nice day for it.
Meow.
Let's get you some breakfast.
Meow.
?
VIRGO
Did you catch this? Or do these things eat cat food, too?
Meow?
VIRGO
I bet you killed it, didn't you?
Meow.
Good cat.
Meow.

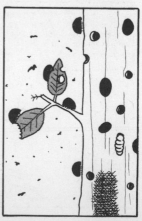

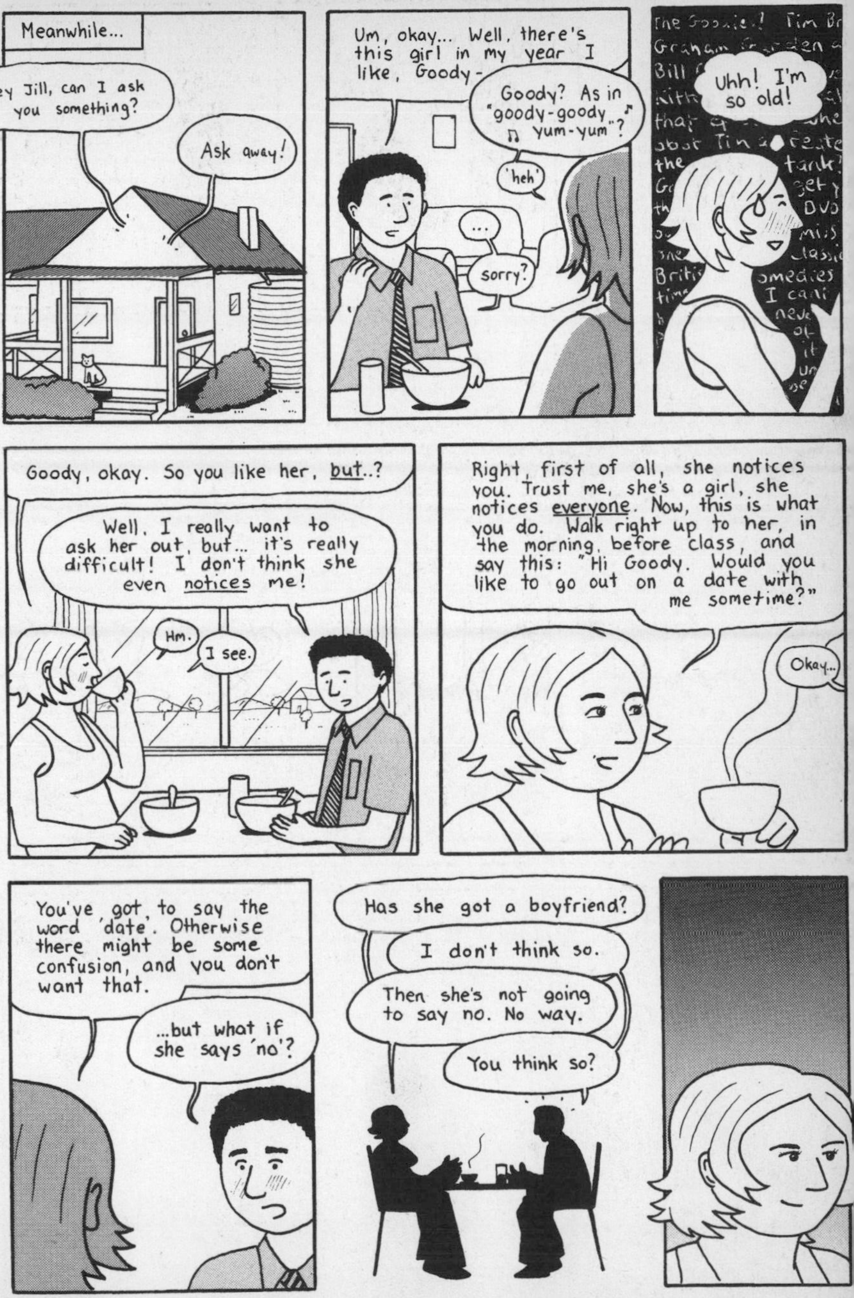
Meanwhile...
Hey Jill, can I ask you something?
Ask away!
Um, okay... Well, there's this girl in my year I like, Goody-
Goody? As in "goody-goody yum-yum"?
'heh'
...
sorry?
Uhh! I'm so old!
Goody, okay. So you like her, but..?
Well, I really want to ask her out, but... it's really difficult! I don't think she even notices me!
Hm.
I see.
Right, first of all, she notices you. Trust me, she's a girl, she notices everyone. Now, this is what you do. Walk right up to her, in the morning, before class, and say this: "Hi Goody. Would you like to go out on a date with me sometime?"
Okay...
You've got to say the word 'date'. Otherwise there might be some confusion, and you don't want that.
...but what if she says 'no'?
Has she got a boyfriend?
I don't think so.
Then she's not going to say no. No way.
You think so?

Here's ten bucks...

...if she says no, take this to the supermarket, buy the richest chocolate ice cream they've got, bring it back here, and eat it with me. Problem solved.

...

...you're a genius.

I know.

Hey.

Hey.

What are you up to today?

Bit of job hunting?

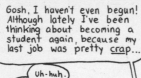

Gosh, I haven't even begun! Although lately I've been thinking about becoming a student again, because my last job was pretty crap...

Uh-huh.

How's it going with the beetle thing?

So-so... they went through another three trees since yesterday. I've burned out as many as I could find, but...

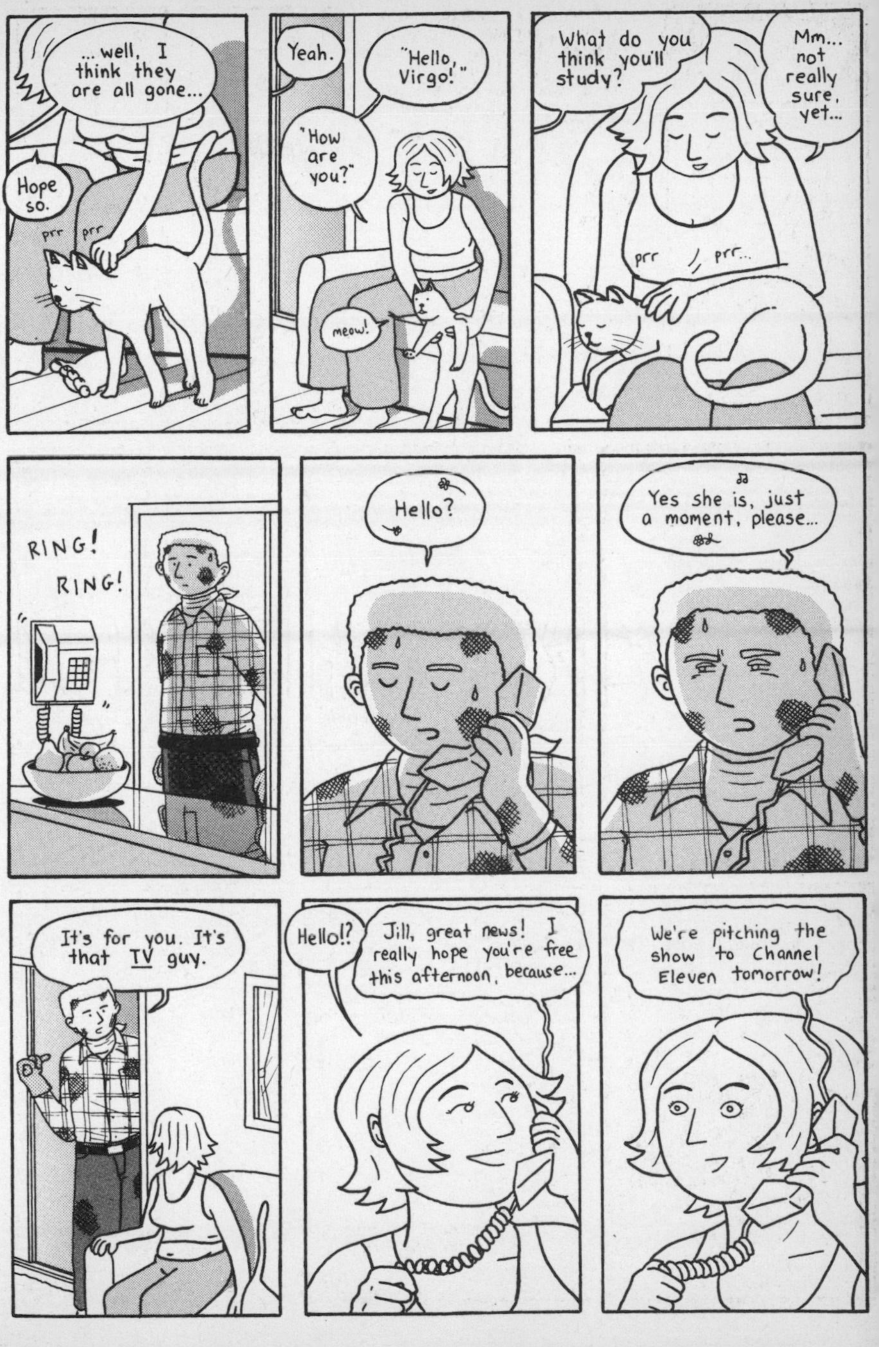

... well, I think they are all gone...
Hope so.
prr prr
Yeah.
"Hello, Virgo!"
"How are you?"
meow!
What do you think you'll study?
Mm... not really sure, yet...
prr prr...
RING!
RING!
Hello?
Yes she is, just a moment, please...
It's for you. It's that TV guy.
Hello!?
Jill, great news! I really hope you're free this afternoon, because...
We're pitching the show to Channel Eleven tomorrow!

Chapter 3

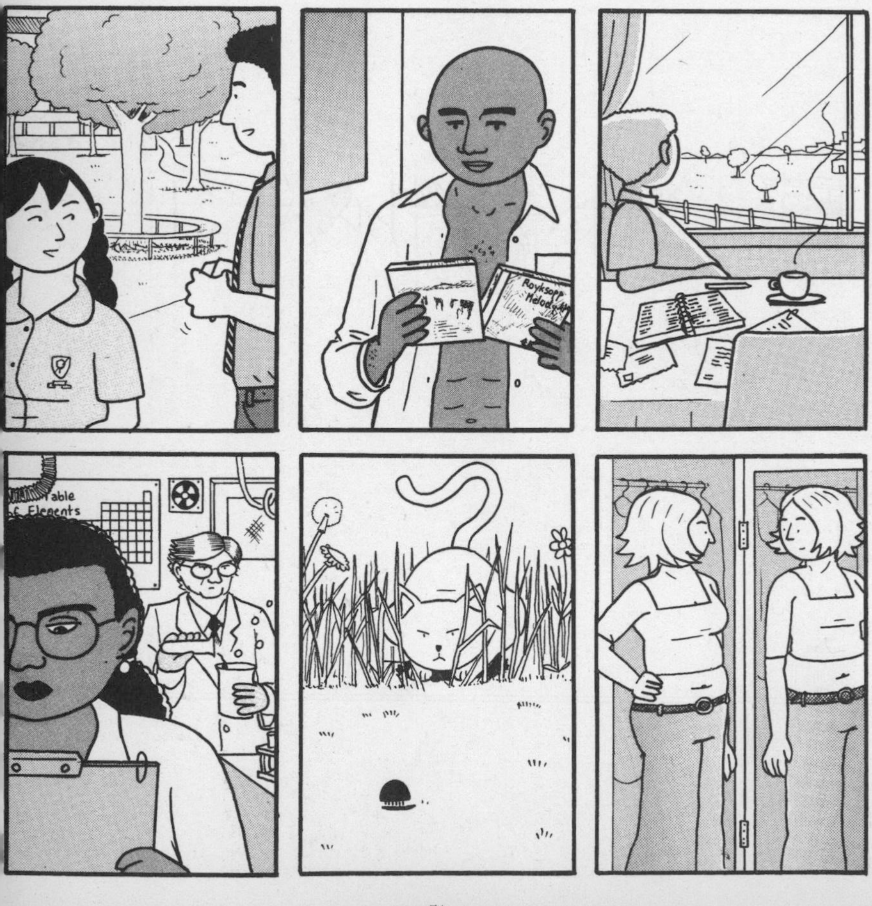
Royksopp

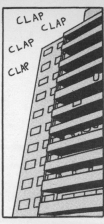

CLAP CLAP
CLAP
CLAP

Jill, we are going to nail this thing tomorrow! I'm totally psyched.

Me too.

Anyway, I think we're ready.

I'm gonna go grab another beer. I need to chill! My thoughts are going a mile a minute...

I can relate. Get me one too.

Okay.

...hey, are you making fun of me?

Yeah,

cuz I think your little catchphrase is stoopid.

Stupid? Stupid is pretending salt and pepper shakers are people,

Jill.

...

You saw that?

Sure. That was one of the things that attracted me to you.

Thanks.

Yeah, I thought you were trying to pick me up.

Well, maybe I was. Too bad you've got a boyfriend, though...

Um

Anyway...

Cheers.

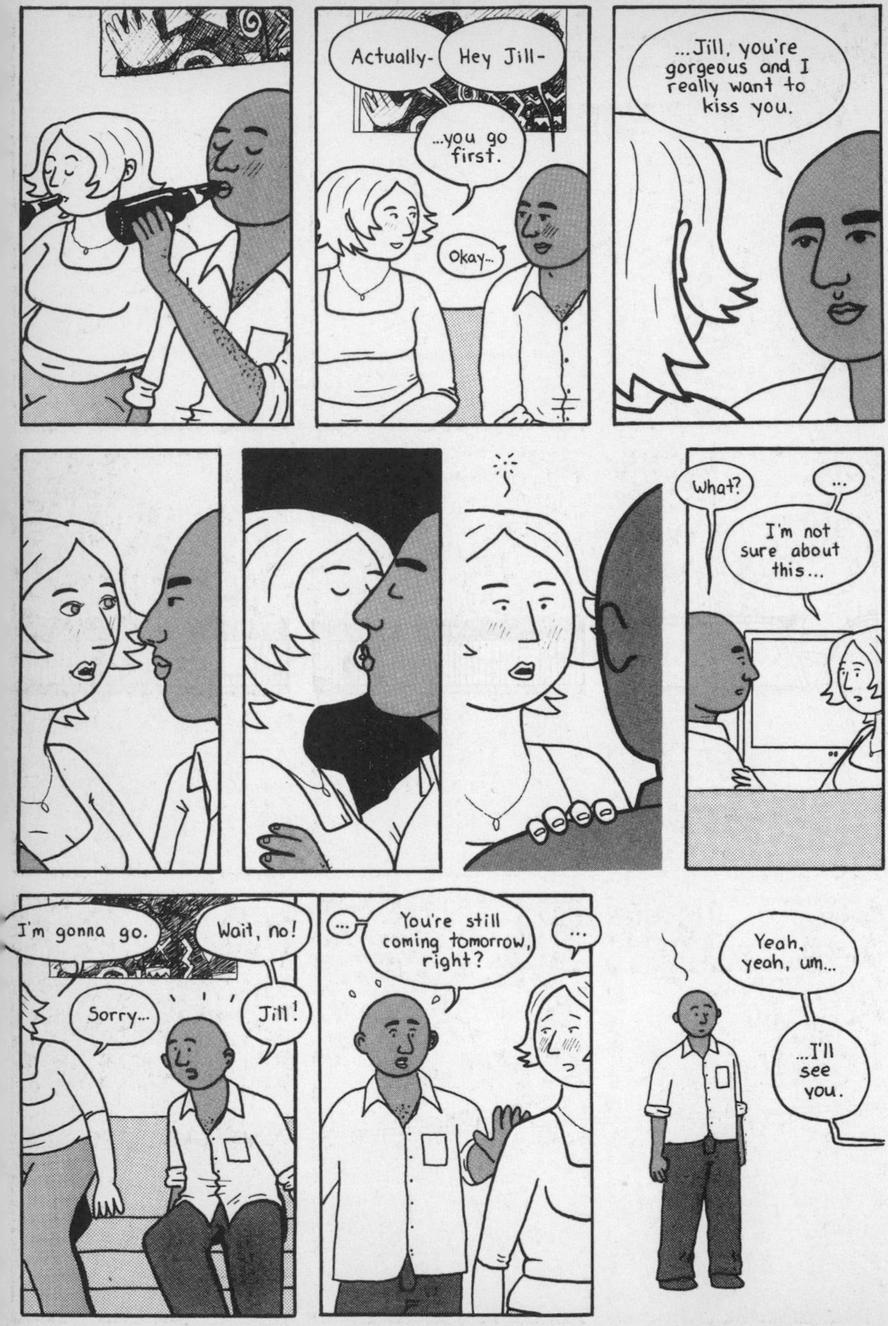
Actually-
Hey Jill-
...you go first.
Okay...
...Jill, you're gorgeous and I really want to kiss you.
What?
...
I'm not sure about this...
I'm gonna go.
Wait, no!
Sorry...
Jill!
...
You're still coming tomorrow, right?
...
Yeah, yeah, um...
...I'll see you.

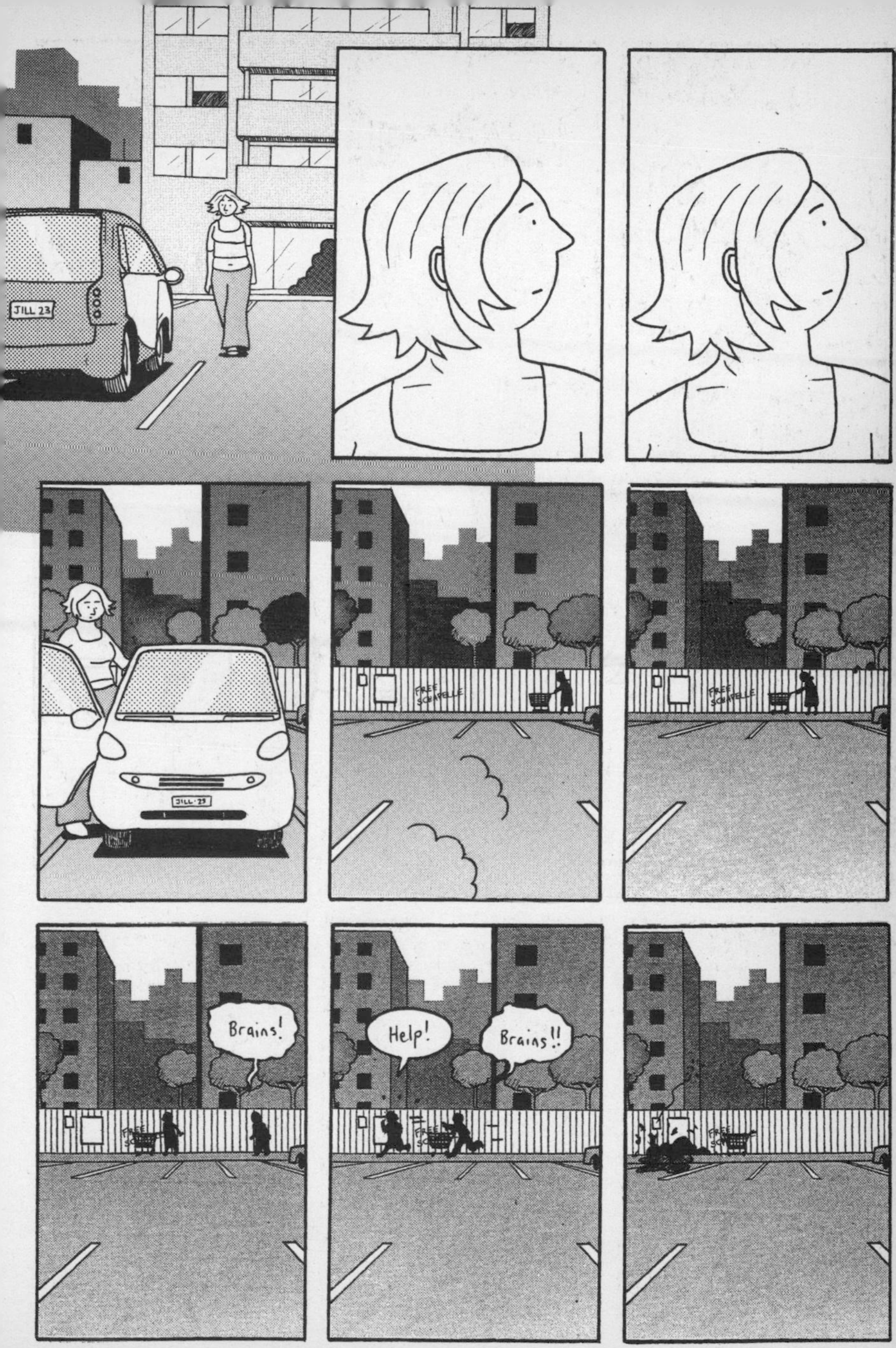
JILL 23
JILL·23
FREE SCHAPELLE
FREE SCHAPELLE
Brains!
Help!
Brains!!

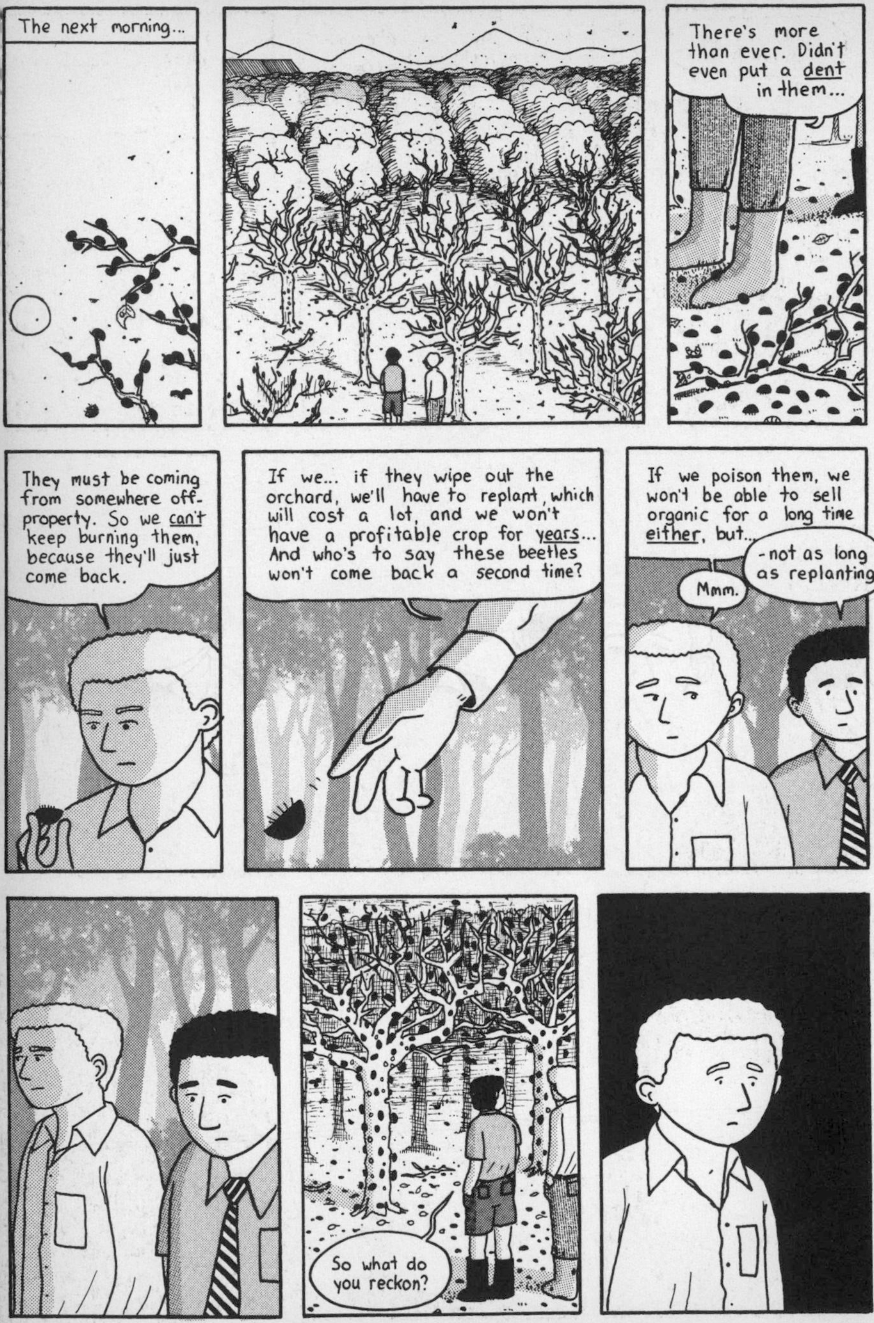

The next morning...
There's more than ever. Didn't even put a dent in them...
They must be coming from somewhere off-property. So we can't keep burning them, because they'll just come back.
If we... if they wipe out the orchard, we'll have to replant, which will cost a lot, and we won't have a profitable crop for years... And who's to say these beetles won't come back a second time?
If we poison them, we won't be able to sell organic for a long time either, but...
Mmm.
-not as long as replanting.
So what do you reckon?

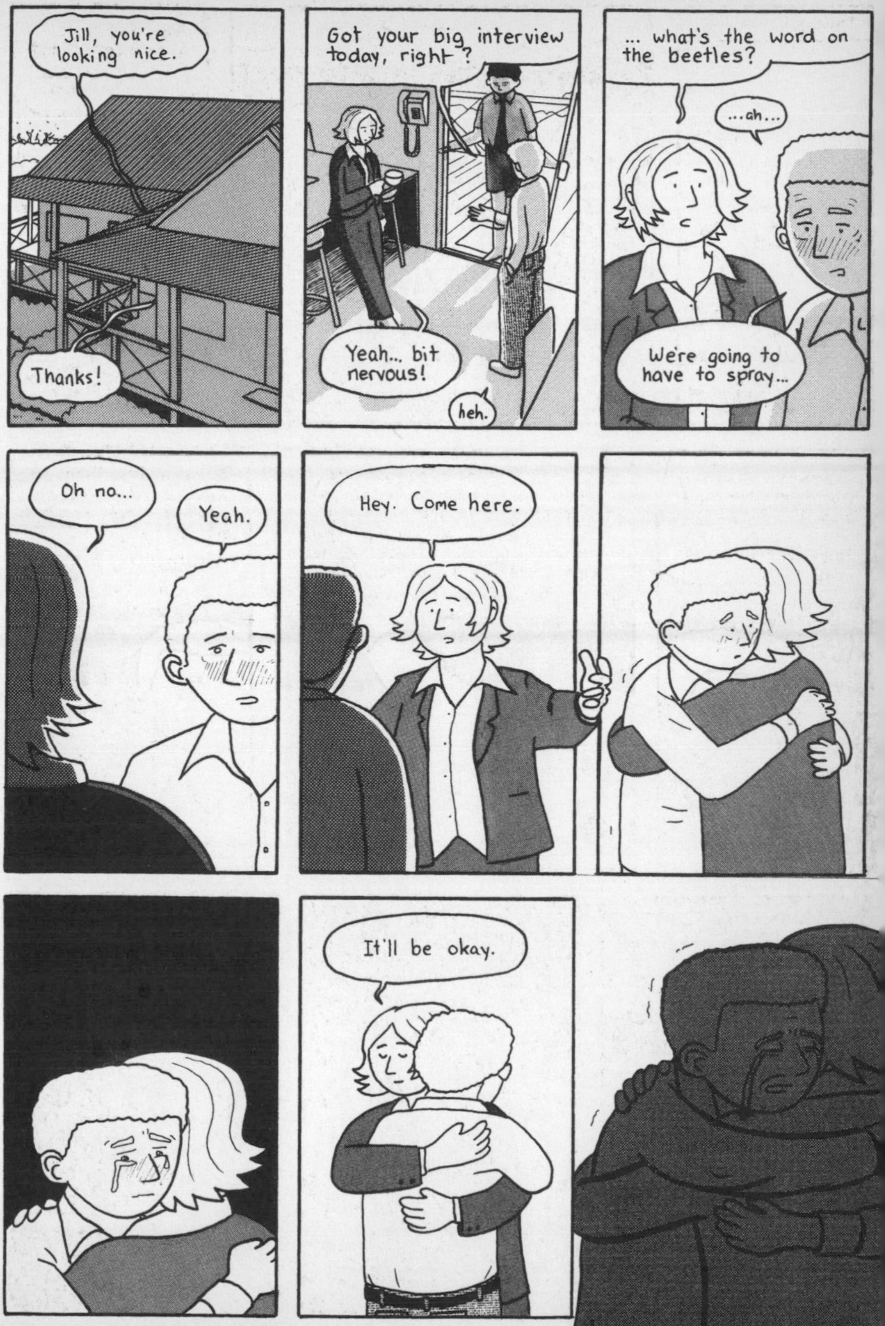
Jill, you're looking nice.
Thanks!
Got your big interview today, right?
Yeah... bit nervous!
heh.
... what's the word on the beetles?
...ah...
We're going to have to spray...
Oh no...
Yeah.
Hey. Come here.
It'll be okay.

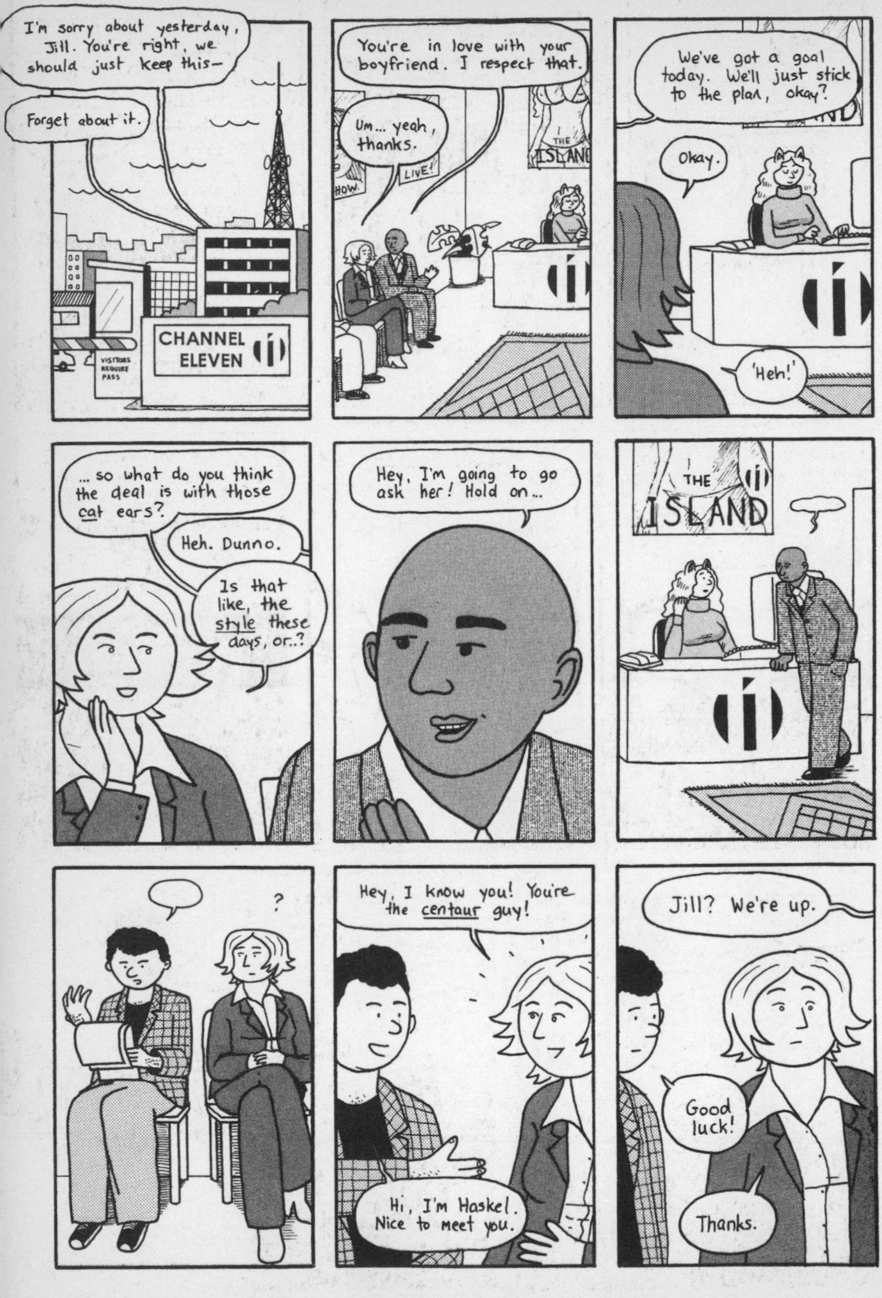
I'm sorry about yesterday, Jill. You're right, we should just keep this—
Forget about it.
CHANNEL ELEVEN
VISITORS REQUIRE PASS
You're in love with your boyfriend. I respect that.
Um... yeah, thanks.
LIVE!
THE ISLAND
We've got a goal today. We'll just stick to the plan, okay?
Okay.
'Heh!'
... so what do you think the deal is with those cat ears?
Heh. Dunno.
Is that like, the style these days, or..?
Hey, I'm going to go ask her! Hold on...
THE ISLAND
?
Hey, I know you! You're the centaur guy!
Hi, I'm Haskel. Nice to meet you.
Jill? We're up.
Good luck!
Thanks.

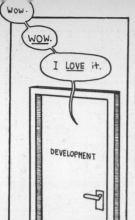

Wow.

WOW.

I LOVE it.

DEVELOPMENT

Me too, this is awesome. So let's talk titles...

Well, *Not In My Backyard* is only a working title.

And I love it, but it's negative and square.

Exactly.

We need to skew to a younger demographic.

How about: "Pollution is a Total Bitch"?

Wow. That is awesome.

Or "Pimp My Environment."

Spectacular!

"Hot, Wet Globe."

Globes.

Love it.

I'd like to sex it up a few grads - how about a hot female presenter?

Blonde, nice bags..

Totally.

...

I'm seeing bikinis.

Yeah, a new one each week! And then we sell 'em on ebay!

Thinkin' outside the box, dude!

Make - you've done it again.

Jill- you rock.

Word.

Welcome. aboard.

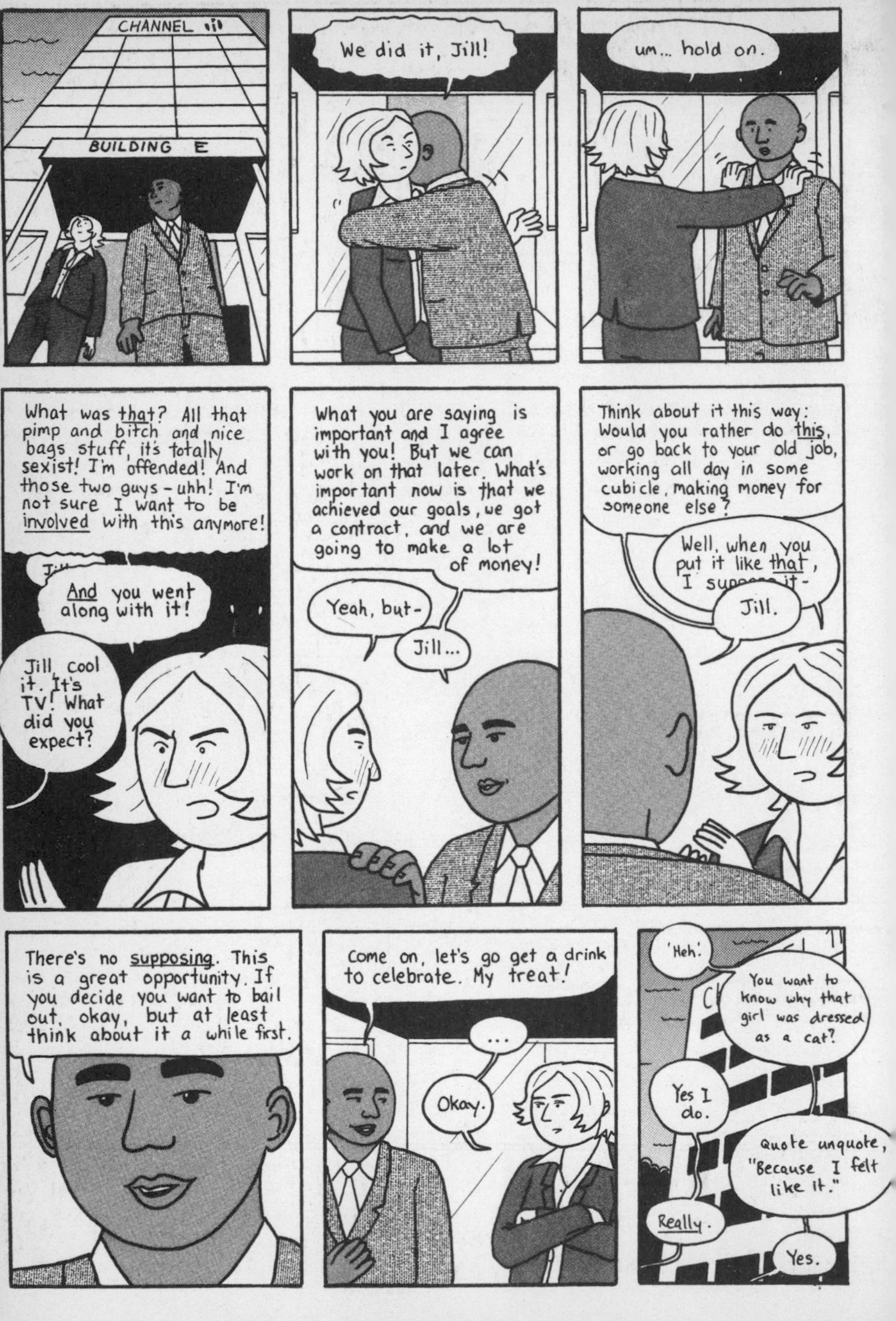
CHANNEL
BUILDING E
We did it, Jill!
um... hold on.
What was that? All that pimp and bitch and nice bags stuff, it's totally sexist! I'm offended! And those two guys - uhh! I'm not sure I want to be involved with this anymore!
And you went along with it!
Jill, cool it. It's TV! What did you expect?
What you are saying is important and I agree with you! But we can work on that later. What's important now is that we achieved our goals, we got a contract, and we are going to make a lot of money!
Yeah, but-
Jill...
Think about it this way: Would you rather do this, or go back to your old job, working all day in some cubicle, making money for someone else?
Well, when you put it like that, I su
Jill.
There's no supposing. This is a great opportunity. If you decide you want to bail out, okay, but at least think about it a while first.
Come on, let's go get a drink to celebrate. My treat!
...
Okay.
'Heh.'
You want to know why that girl was dressed as a cat?
Yes I do.
Quote unquote, "Because I felt like it."
Really.
Yes.

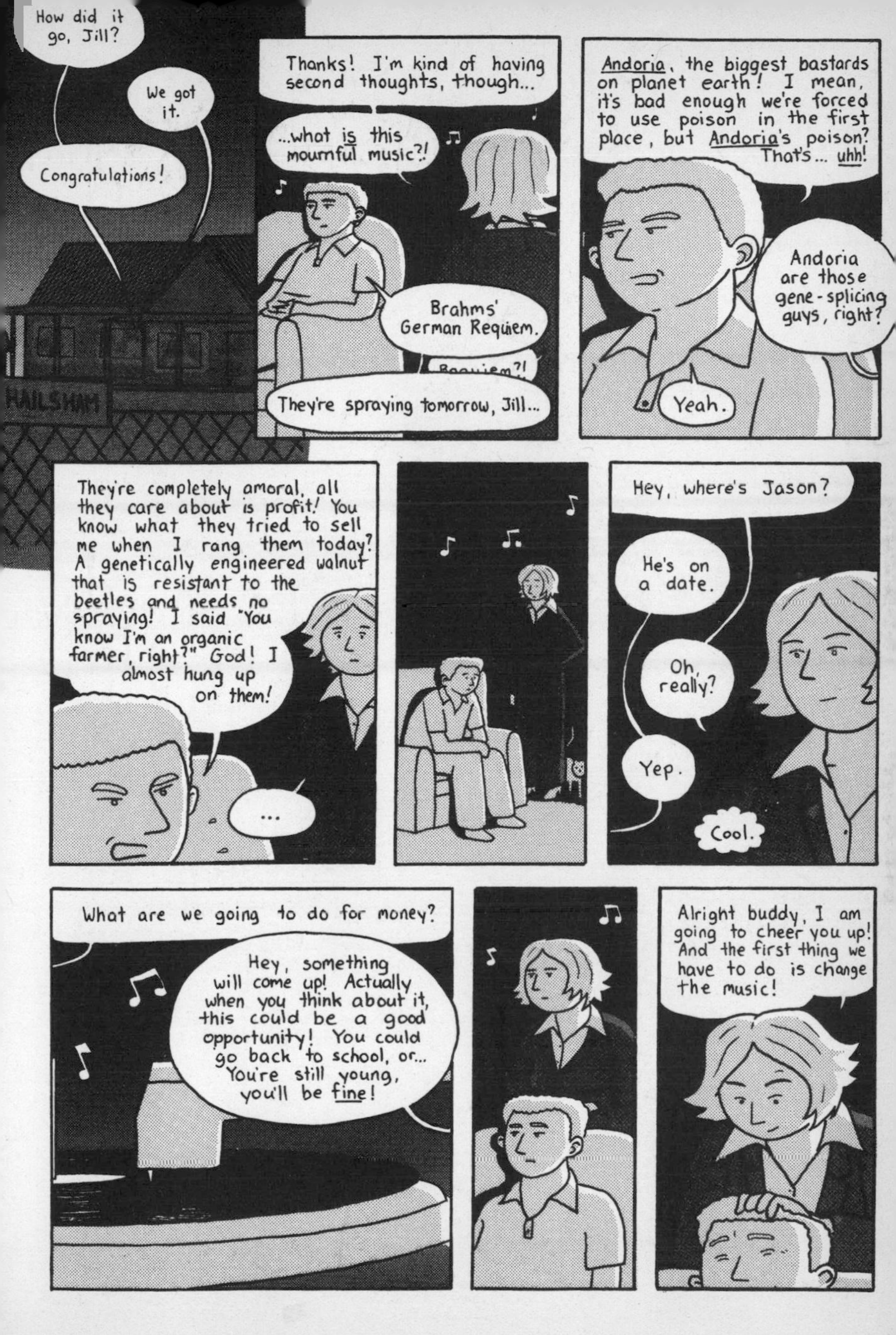

How did it go, Jill?
We got it.
Congratulations!
Thanks! I'm kind of having second thoughts, though...
...what is this mournful music?!
Brahms' German Requiem.
They're spraying tomorrow, Jill...
Andoria, the biggest bastards on planet earth! I mean, it's bad enough we're forced to use poison in the first place, but Andoria's poison? That's... uhh!
Andoria are those gene-splicing guys, right?
Yeah.
They're completely amoral, all they care about is profit! You know what they tried to sell me when I rang them today? A genetically engineered walnut that is resistant to the beetles and needs no spraying! I said "You know I'm an organic farmer, right?" God! I almost hung up on them!
...
Hey, where's Jason?
He's on a date.
Oh, really?
Yep.
Cool.
What are we going to do for money?
Hey, something will come up! Actually when you think about it, this could be a good opportunity! You could go back to school, or... You're still young, you'll be fine!
Alright buddy, I am going to cheer you up! And the first thing we have to do is change the music!

Earlier, in Washington, D.C...
The situation is critical, Mr. President...
91% of victims are Caucasian, and 60% are in the USA alone. The disease strikes at random, and is as yet irreversible.
INCIDENCES OF
projected
actual
Ooo-ee!
As this gr
reports of
of MHD
almost dai
trend con
...Western
could
within
Mostly Americans, you say? White folks?
That's correct, sir.
I think I know where you're going with this, sir. And no, Al-Qaeda is almost certainly not responsible for MHD.
If I may, sir-this threat is more dangerous than terrorism, and requires strong, immediate action from the administration!
...Mr. President?
...
BRAINS!

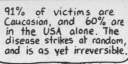

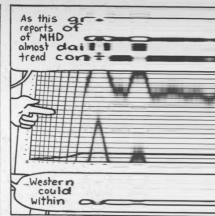

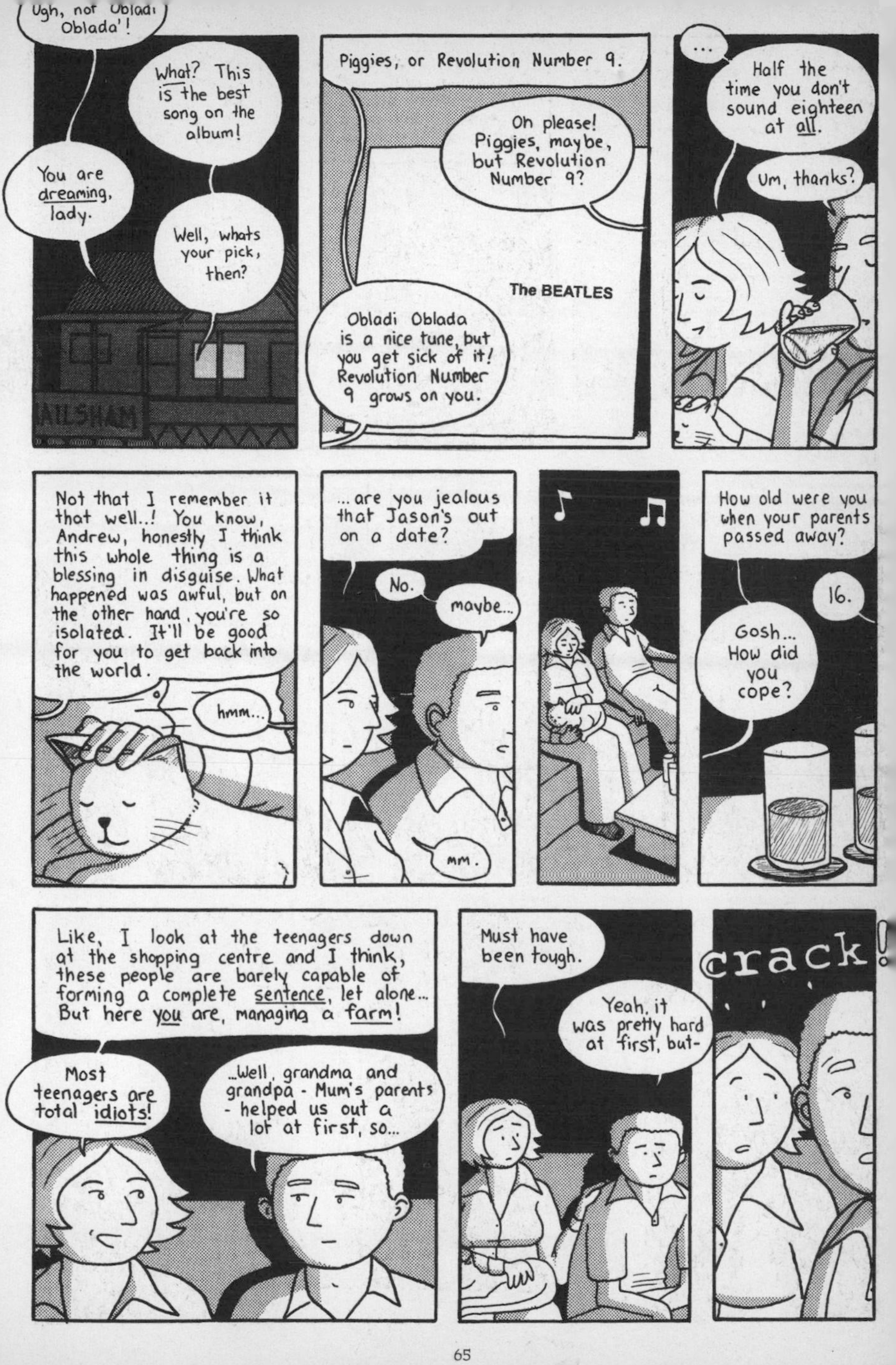

Ugh, not Obladi Oblada'!
What? This is the best song on the album!
You are dreaming, lady.
Well, whats your pick, then?
AILSHAM
Piggies, or Revolution Number 9.
Oh please! Piggies, maybe, but Revolution Number 9?
The BEATLES
Obladi Oblada is a nice tune, but you get sick of it! Revolution Number 9 grows on you.
...
Half the time you don't sound eighteen at all.
Um, thanks?
Not that I remember it that well..! You know, Andrew, honestly I think this whole thing is a blessing in disguise. What happened was awful, but on the other hand, you're so isolated. It'll be good for you to get back into the world.
hmm...
... are you jealous that Jason's out on a date?
No.
maybe...
mm.
How old were you when your parents passed away?
16.
Gosh... How did you cope?
Like, I look at the teenagers down at the shopping centre and I think, these people are barely capable of forming a complete sentence, let alone... But here you are, managing a farm!
Most teenagers are total idiots!
...Well, grandma and grandpa - Mum's parents - helped us out a lot at first, so...
Must have been tough.
Yeah, it was pretty hard at first, but-
crack!

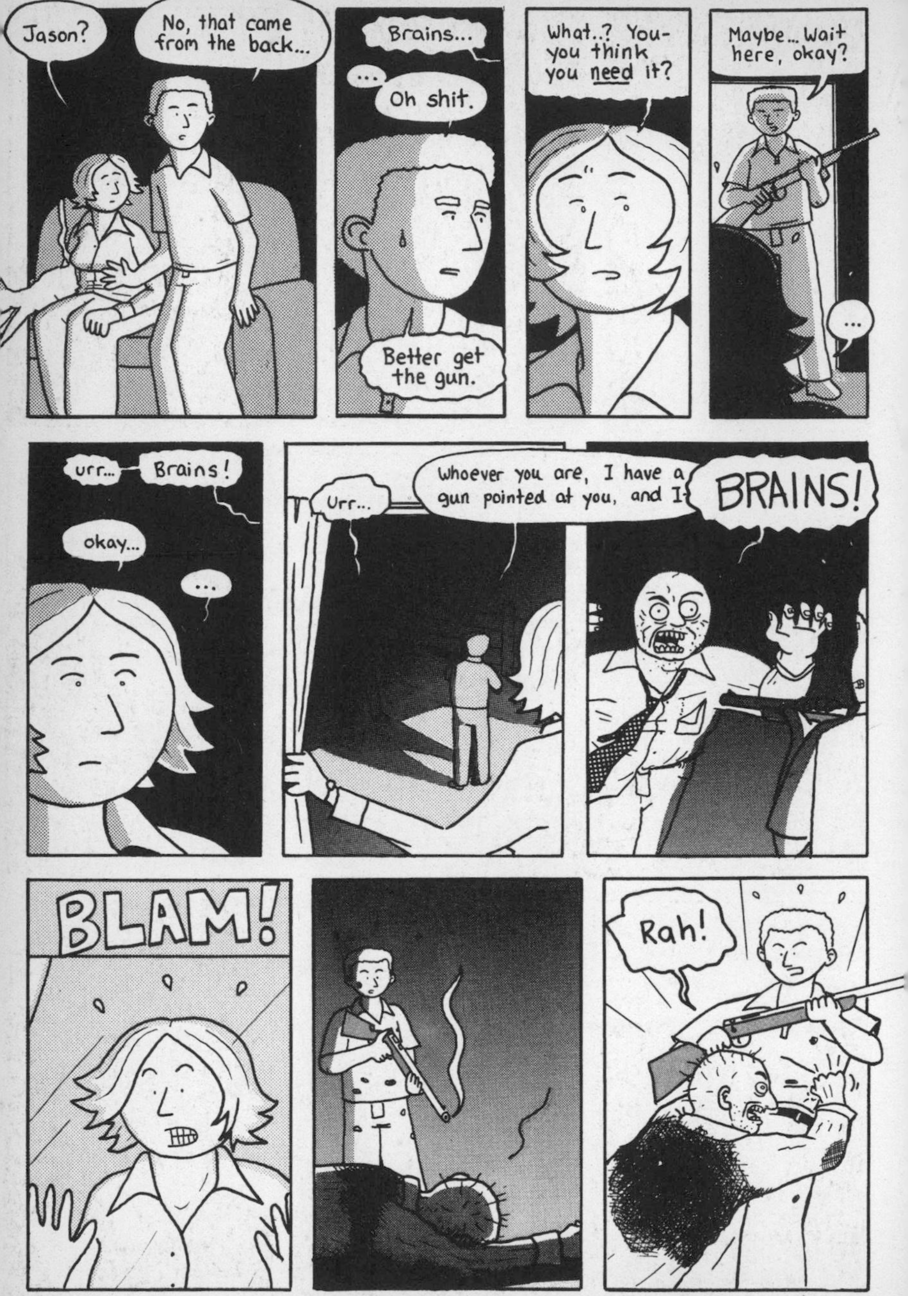

Jason?
No, that came from the back...
Brains...
...
Oh shit.
Better get the gun.
What..? You- you think you need it?
Maybe... Wait here, okay?
...
urr...
Brains!
okay...
...
Urr...
Whoever you are, I have a gun pointed at you, and I-
BRAINS!
BLAM!
Rah!

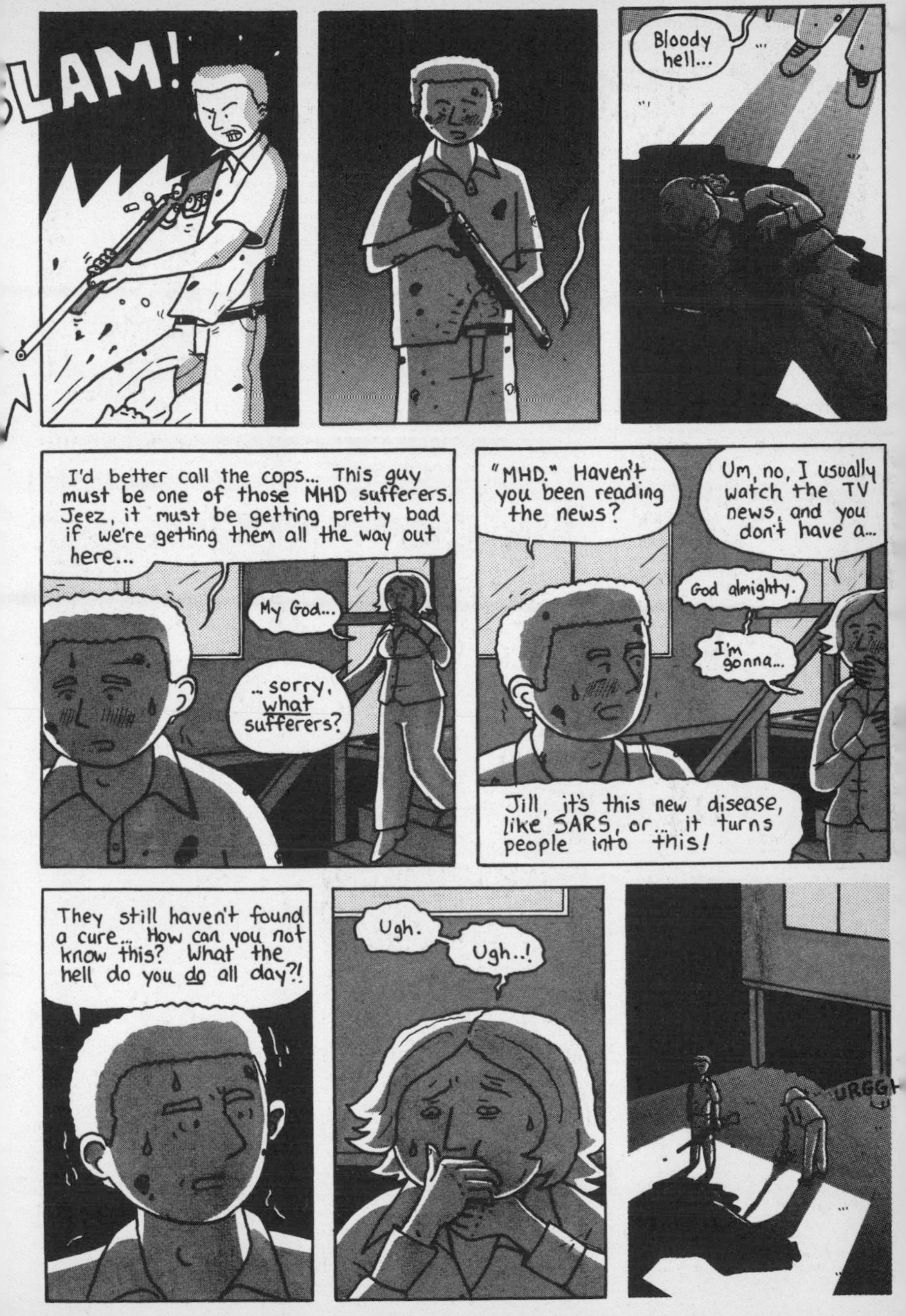
SLAM!
Bloody hell...
I'd better call the cops... This guy must be one of those MHD sufferers. Jeez, it must be getting pretty bad if we're getting them all the way out here...
My God...
... sorry, what sufferers?
"MHD." Haven't you been reading the news?
Um, no, I usually watch the TV news, and you don't have a...
God almighty.
I'm gonna...
Jill, it's this new disease, like SARS, or... it turns people into this!
They still haven't found a cure... How can you not know this? What the hell do you do all day?!
Ugh.
Ugh..!
URGG

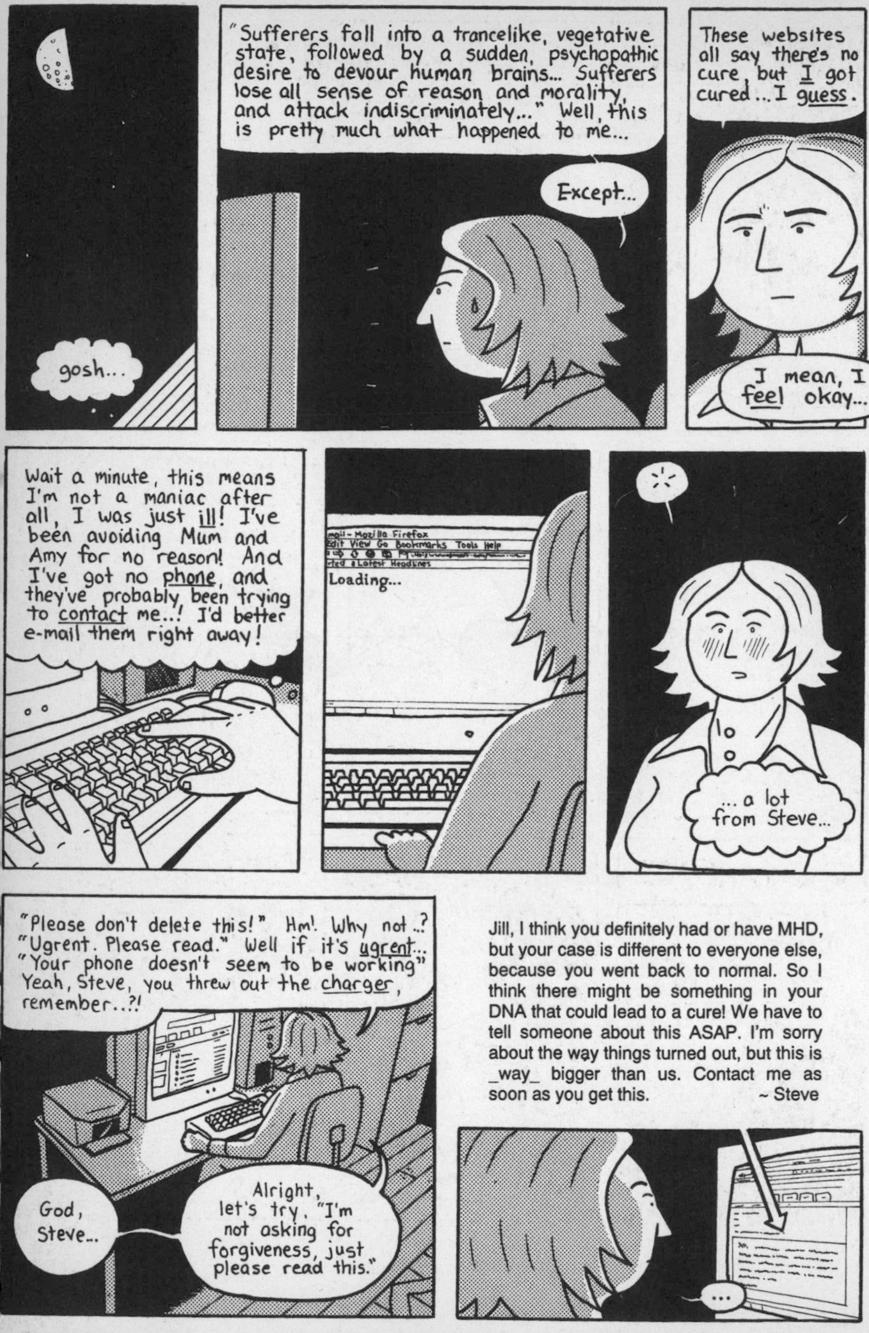
gosh...
"Sufferers fall into a trancelike, vegetative state, followed by a sudden, psychopathic desire to devour human brains... Sufferers lose all sense of reason and morality, and attack indiscriminately..." Well, this is pretty much what happened to me...
Except...
These websites all say there's no cure, but I got cured... I guess.
I mean, I feel okay...
Wait a minute, this means I'm not a maniac after all, I was just ill! I've been avoiding Mum and Amy for no reason! And I've got no phone, and they've probably been trying to contact me...! I'd better e-mail them right away!
Edit View Go Bookmarks Tools Help
Loading...
... a lot from Steve...
"Please don't delete this!" Hm! Why not..? "Ugrent. Please read." Well if it's ugrent... "Your phone doesn't seem to be working" Yeah, Steve, you threw out the charger, remember...?!
God, Steve...
Alright, let's try, "I'm not asking for forgiveness, just please read this."
Jill, I think you definitely had or have MHD, but your case is different to everyone else, because you went back to normal. So I think there might be something in your DNA that could lead to a cure! We have to tell someone about this ASAP. I'm sorry about the way things turned out, but this is _way_ bigger than us. Contact me as soon as you get this. ~ Steve
...

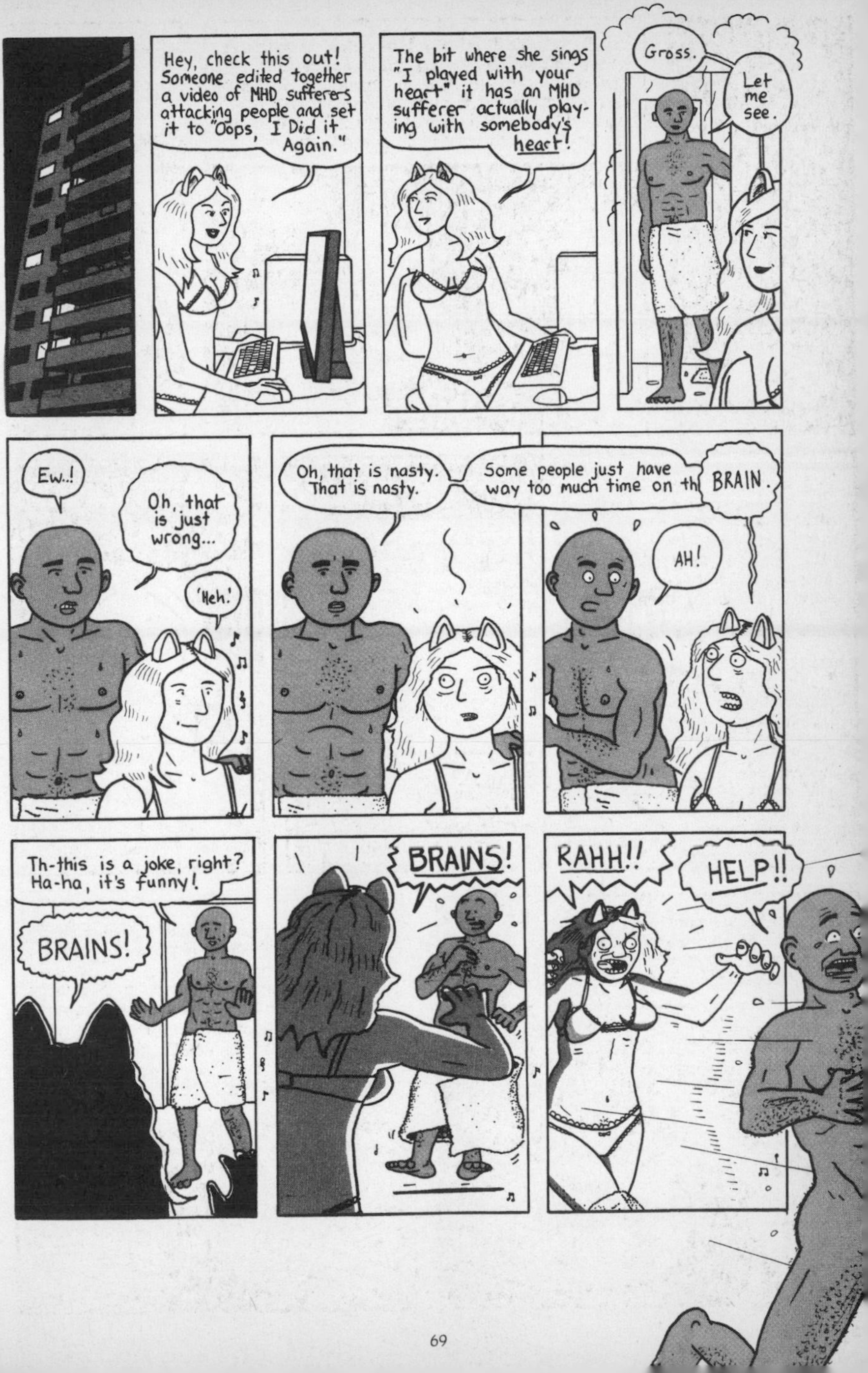
Hey, check this out! Someone edited together a video of MHD sufferers attacking people and set it to "Oops, I Did it Again."
The bit where she sings "I played with your heart" it has an MHD sufferer actually playing with somebody's heart!
Gross.
Let me see.
Ew..!
Oh, that is just wrong...
'Heh.'
Oh, that is nasty. That is nasty.
Some people just have way too much time on th
BRAIN.
AH!
Th-this is a joke, right? Ha-ha, it's funny!
BRAINS!
BRAINS!
RAHH!!
HELP!!

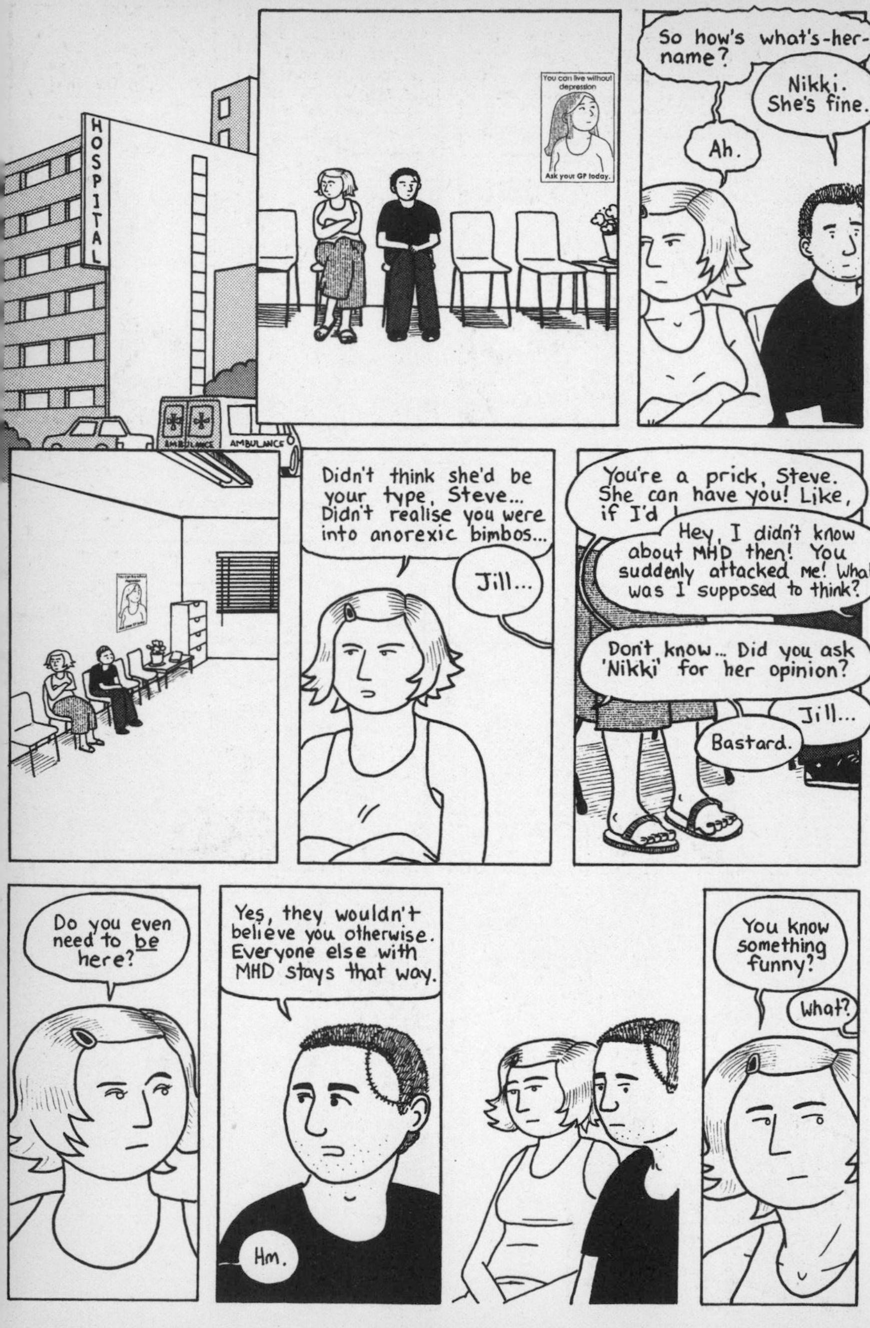
HOSPITAL
AMBULANCE
AMBULANCE
You can live without depression
Ask your GP today.
So how's what's-her-name?
Nikki. She's fine.
Ah.
Didn't think she'd be your type, Steve... Didn't realise you were into anorexic bimbos...
Jill...
You're a prick, Steve. She can have you! Like, if I'd
Hey, I didn't know about MHD then! You suddenly attacked me! What was I supposed to think?
Don't know... Did you ask 'Nikki' for her opinion?
Jill...
Bastard.
Do you even need to be here?
Yes, they wouldn't believe you otherwise. Everyone else with MHD stays that way.
Hm.
You know something funny?
What?

I had a weird thought the other day. I thought that maybe the whole head-biting incident was just a fantasy I'd conjured to deal with our break-up. Because it didn't seem real! But it all became crystal clear after last night...

How is that funny?

...

Oh... yeah, I guess that isn't that funny...

Hey, I thought the doctor said your personality would be **different**... but you seem pretty normal to me.

Yeah. They gave me some pills for that.

Ah.

Ms. Fox, Mr. Bagdasarian? The doctor will see you now.

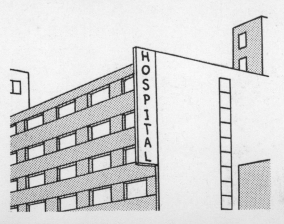

HOSPITAL

Epilogue

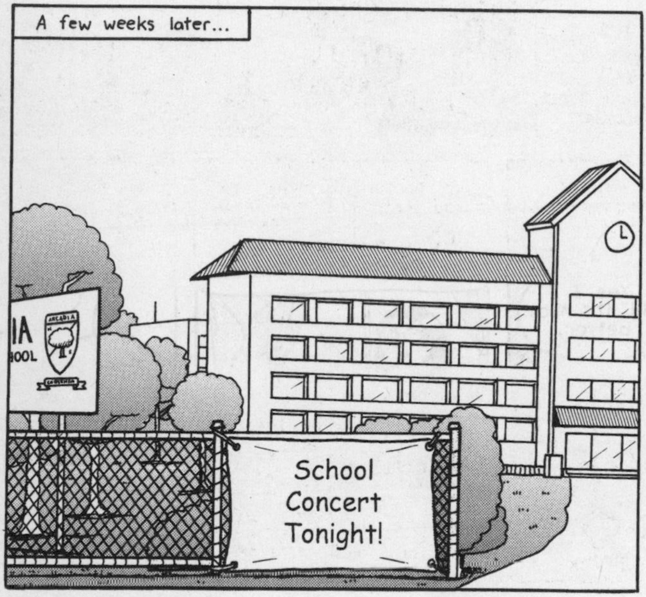
A few weeks later...
School Concert Tonight!

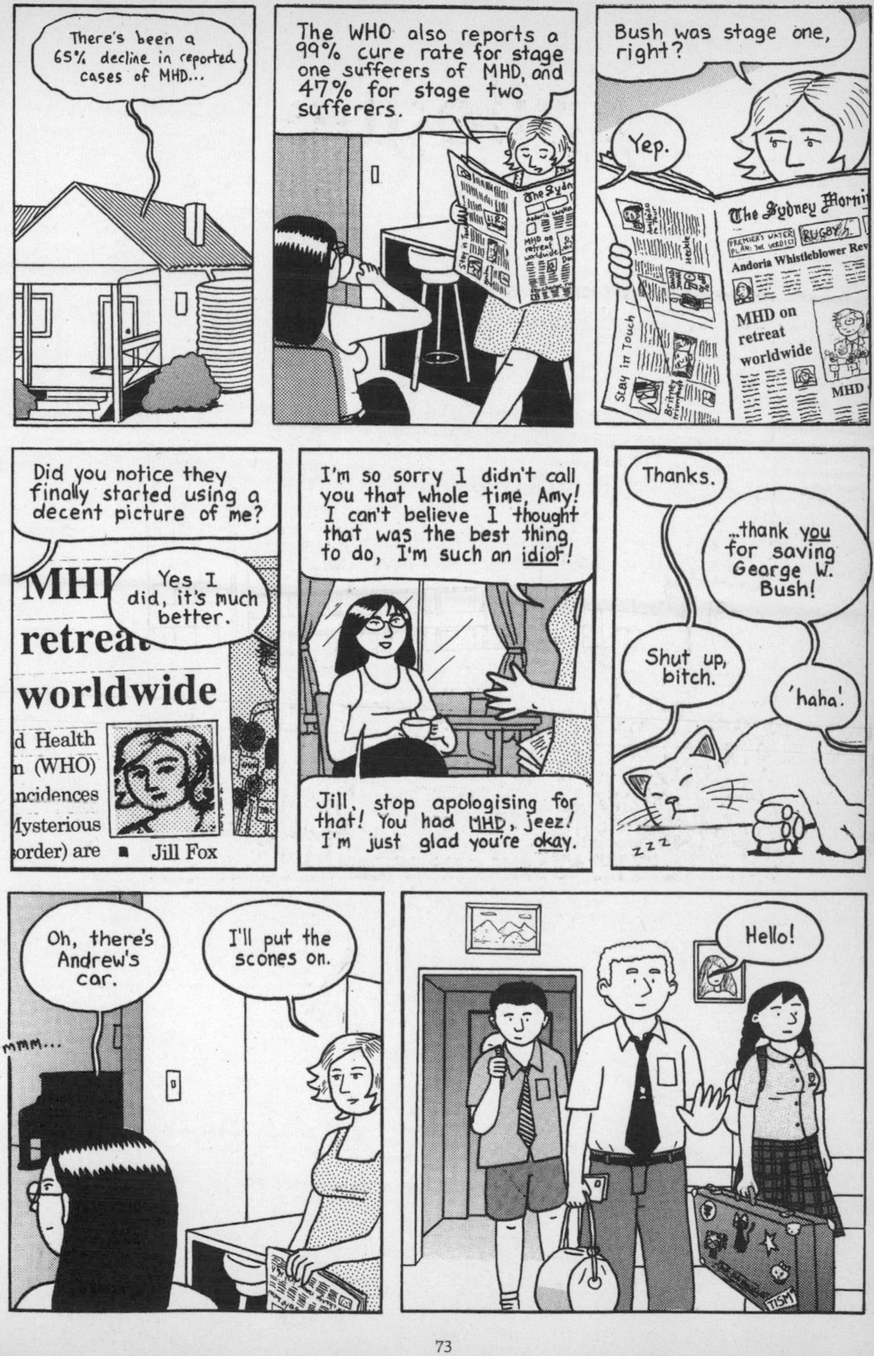
There's been a 65% decline in reported cases of MHD...
The WHO also reports a 99% cure rate for stage one sufferers of MHD, and 47% for stage two sufferers.
Bush was stage one, right?
Yep.
The Sydney Mornin
PREMIER'S WATER PLAN: THE VERDICT
RUGBY
Andoria Whistleblower Rev
MHD on retreat worldwide
Stay in Touch
Heckle
MHD
Did you notice they finally started using a decent picture of me?
Yes I did, it's much better.
MHD
retreat
worldwide
d Health
n (WHO)
ncidences
Mysterious
sorder) are
Jill Fox
I'm so sorry I didn't call you that whole time, Amy! I can't believe I thought that was the best thing to do, I'm such an idiot!
Jill, stop apologising for that! You had MHD, jeez! I'm just glad you're okay.
Thanks.
...thank you for saving George W. Bush!
Shut up, bitch.
'haha'.
zzz
vrmmm...
Oh, there's Andrew's car.
I'll put the scones on.
Hello!
TISM

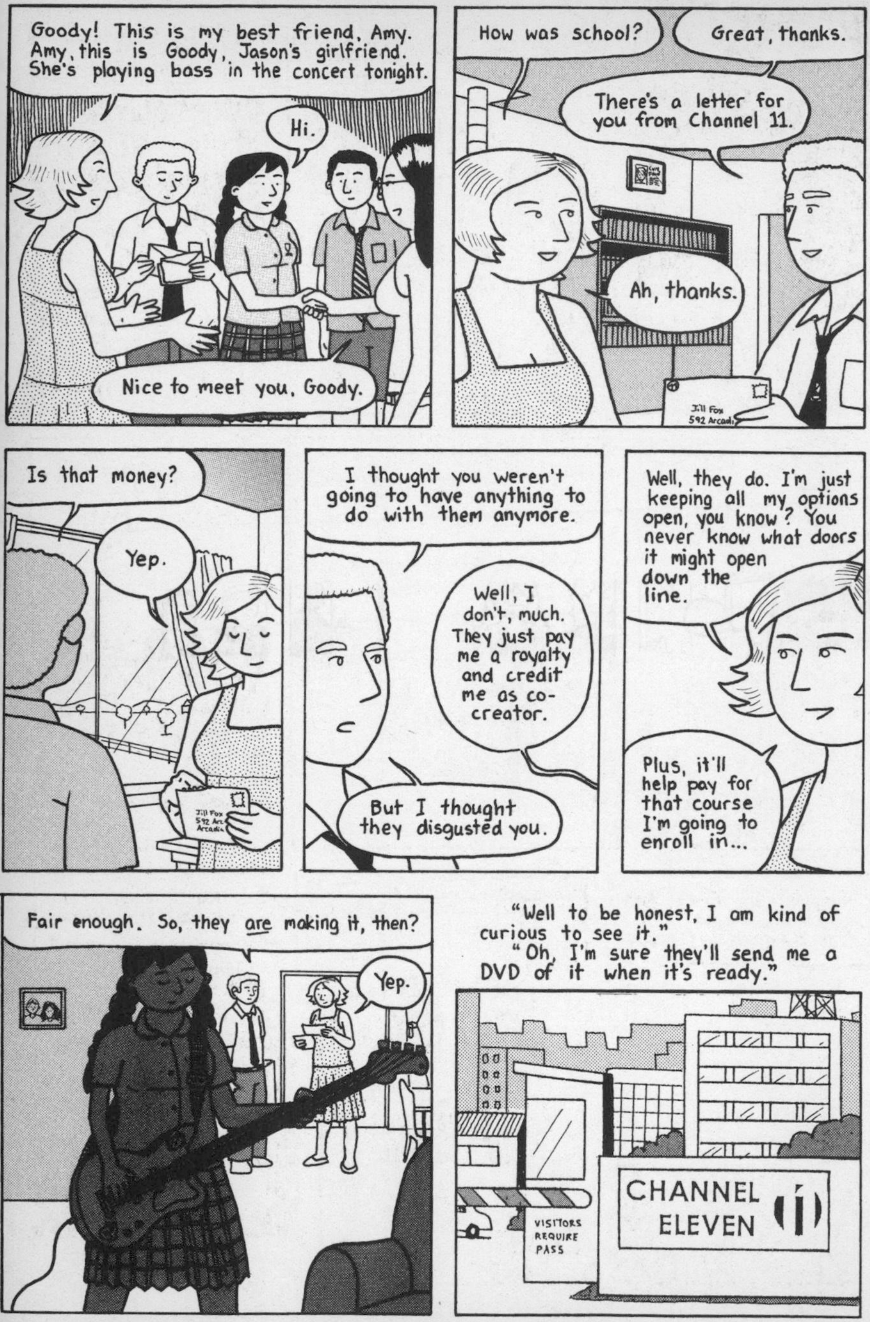
Goody! This is my best friend, Amy. Amy, this is Goody, Jason's girlfriend. She's playing bass in the concert tonight.
Hi.
Nice to meet you, Goody.
How was school?
Great, thanks.
There's a letter for you from Channel 11.
Ah, thanks.
Jill Fox
Is that money?
Yep.
I thought you weren't going to have anything to do with them anymore.
Well, I don't, much. They just pay me a royalty and credit me as co-creator.
But I thought they disgusted you.
Well, they do. I'm just keeping all my options open, you know? You never know what doors it might open down the line.
Plus, it'll help pay for that course I'm going to enroll in...
Fair enough. So, they are making it, then?
Yep.
"Well to be honest, I am kind of curious to see it."
"Oh, I'm sure they'll send me a DVD of it when it's ready."
VISITORS REQUIRE PASS
CHANNEL ELEVEN

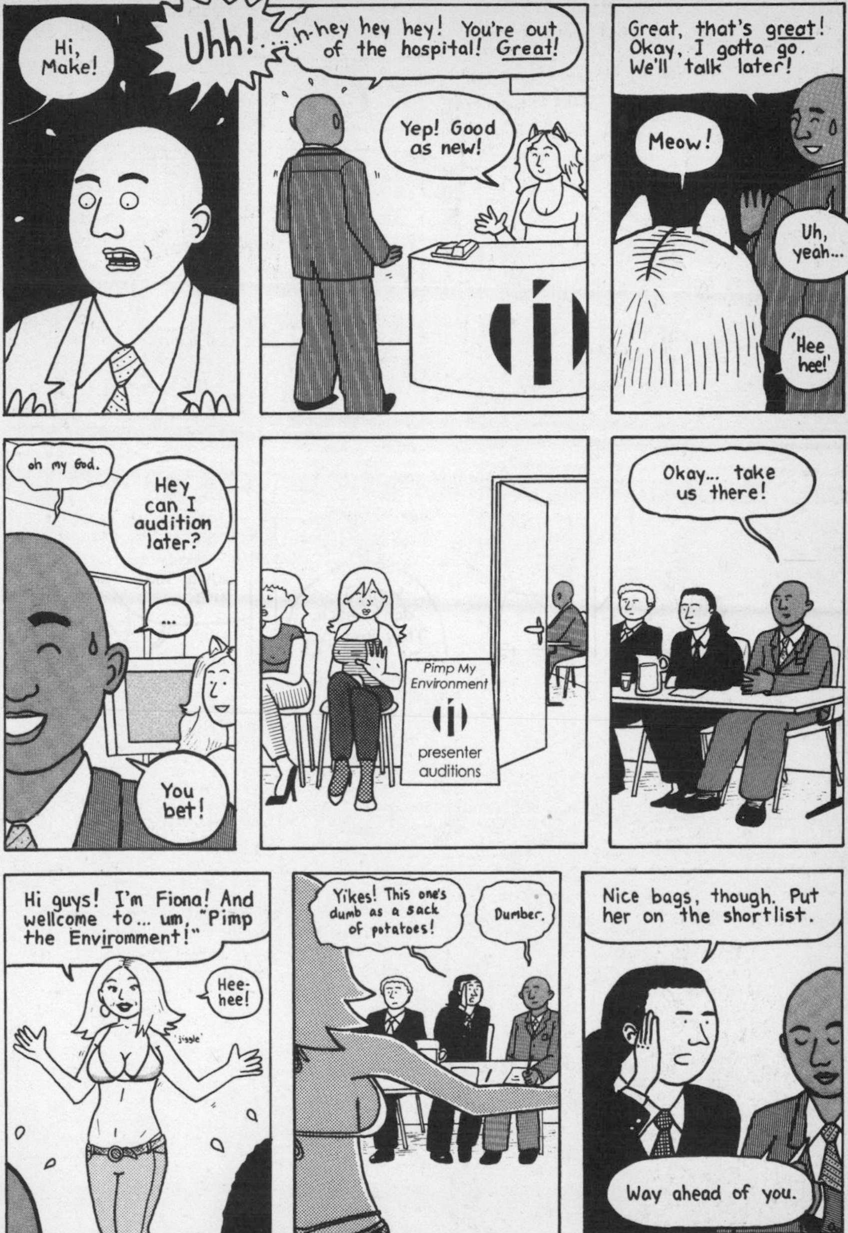
Hi, Make!
Uhh!
...h-hey hey hey! You're out of the hospital! Great!
Yep! Good as new!
Great, that's great! Okay, I gotta go. We'll talk later!
Meow!
Uh, yeah...
'Hee hee!'
oh my God.
Hey can I audition later?
...
You bet!
Pimp My Environment
presenter auditions
Okay... take us there!
Hi guys! I'm Fiona! And wellcome to... um, "Pimp the Enviromment!"
Hee-hee!
'jiggle'
Yikes! This one's dumb as a sack of potatoes!
Dumber.
Nice bags, though. Put her on the shortlist.
Way ahead of you.

"Girls can do anything,
you can pass the test,"

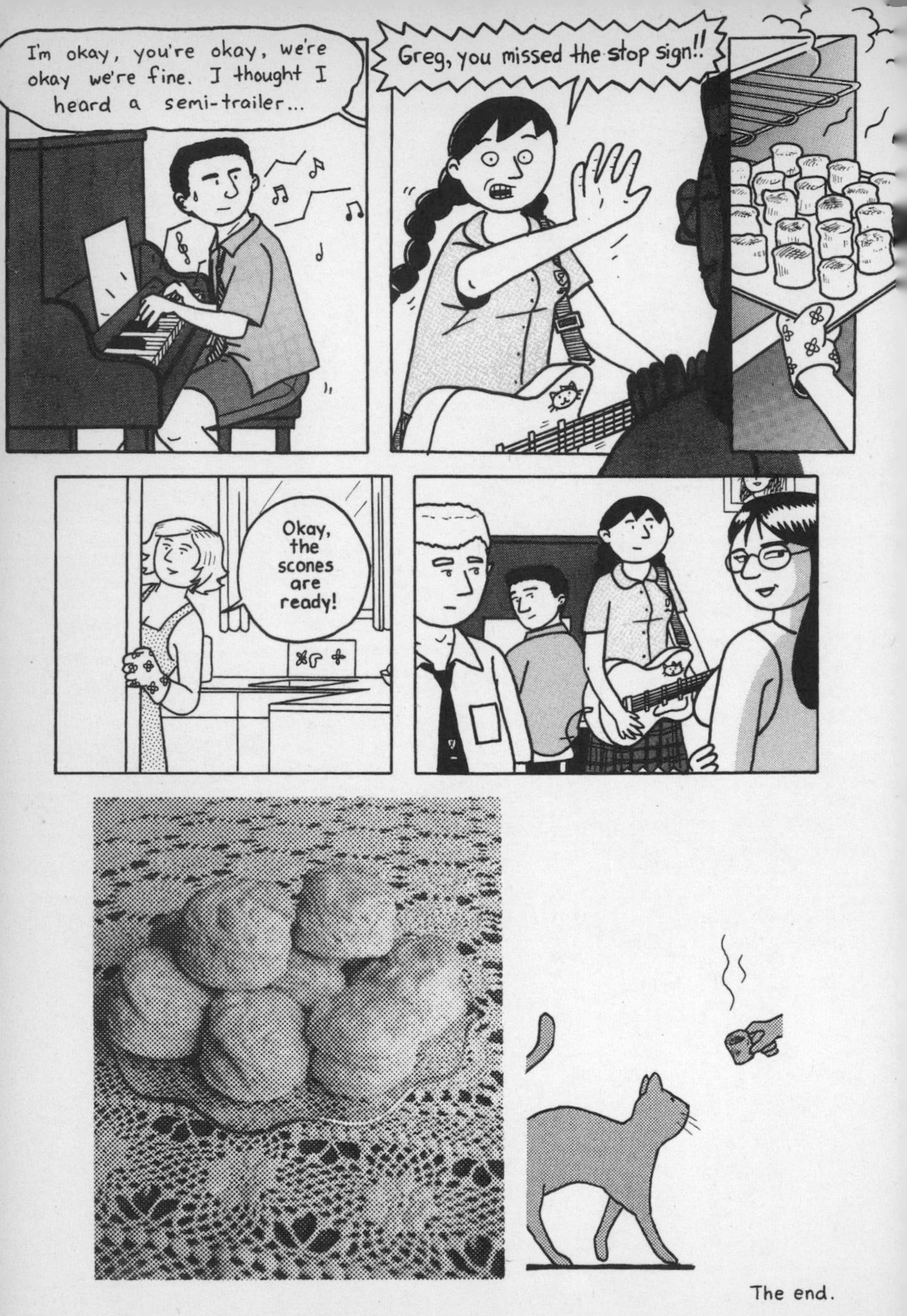
I'm okay, you're okay, we're okay we're fine. I thought I heard a semi-trailer...
Greg, you missed the stop sign!!
Okay, the scones are ready!
The end.

J. Marc Schmidt was born in Sydney, Australia, on September 4, 1973. He is the second of three brothers. After graduating from university, he worked as a substitute high school teacher for a few years. Then he got a job as an English teacher in South Korea. In Korea, he got the idea for *Egg Story*, which was published by SLG in 2004. The same year, Marc went to Germany, to study and teach English again. After that he lived and taught English in Australia again, then Japan for a year. In between all that moving and teaching, he drew *Eating Steve*. He's contributed to anthologies published by SLG, Blackglass Press, and Cardigan Comics, is the artist of the webcomic *Nannah Laveaux*, and is the author of a forthcoming collection of essays, *Secrets of Popular Culture*.

Photo by Andrew Blythe.